WRITERS REPUBLIC

RISING
PHOENIX

Controlling the Flames, Cooling the Embers
and Rising from the Ashes

TARREKA GARNETT

WRITERS REPUBLIC L.L.C.
515 Summit Ave. Unit R1
Union City, NJ 07087, USA

Website: *www.writersrepublic.com*
Hotline: *1-877-656-6838*
Email: *info@writersrepublic.com*

Ordering Information:
Quantity sales. Special discounts are available on quantity purchases by corporations, associations, and others. For details, contact the publisher at the address above.

Library of Congress Control Number:		2022933135	
ISBN-13:	979-8-88536-020-3	[Paperback Edition]
	979-8-88536-021-0	[Hardback Edition]
	979-8-88536-022-7	[Digital Edition]

Rev. date: 02/16/2022

Dedication

This book is dedicated to my daughter Raiyah. Being your mother motivates me to be the best version of myself I can be. I wrote this book so that you would know how hard I am working to be the mother you deserve. I love you more than you can ever imagine, and I hope you grow to accomplish everything you set your mind to.

I want to also dedicate this book to my cousin Tanaji Garnett. Crohn's Disease took you away from us too soon! Your memory will forever live on in our hearts and I will continue to chase my dreams, because you didn't get a chance to accomplish yours. Sleep well cousin... I have it from here!

Foreword

I have learned that there are no magic wands, magic spells, or secret formulas that will propel you to a lifetime of success. The only road map to success is a willingness to set a goal, work hard, and stay the course throughout the journey. Frankly, I am intrigued when I meet a young person who is motivated, established, and passionate about their future. Although I am not always privy to the way they began their journey, I am thrilled for what's to come! As an educator with more than twenty years of experience in working with at-risk youth, I have found it necessary to affirm my students by validating their stories.

It is important to listen when young people share thoughts about their feelings, emotions, and beliefs. This ensures them they are seen and heard. No matter how troubled or challenged a child appears, they all have something valuable to add to society. It is imperative that young people are taught at an early age to believe in themselves, despite their demographic position or socioeconomic status. Moreover, it is beneficial to their self-esteem and to the progression of their self-awareness. Consequently, it's the self-awareness that helps them to evolve and ultimately become what has been predestined for their future.

Life events continually happens to each one of us, and it is rare to find someone who has not been impacted by the drudgeries of life. However, I celebrate those who are victorious despite the challenges that they have faced! I am fascinated by those who rise and declare the victory over their lives, regardless of their formidable journey!

This book will motivate any person who has struggled with intrinsic motivation at some point in their life. It is a refreshing take on life, love of self, and the release of strongholds that endeavor to keep one stuck in a position of complacency. It is a written by a truth-teller and visionary who has used her gift to exalt those who are ready to soar! Enjoy!

Tonjeria Clark Hammond
Counselor/Educator
M.S. Guidance and Counseling K-12

Preface

Are You Stopping You?

It took thirty-six years for me to realize that the protagonist in my life's story was me. After a childhood of abandonment, abuse, and poverty, I created an image of my future that was cloaked in happiness and success; and I wanted nothing more than to get to a place in my life where I could finally experience continued and sustained joy. When I turned eighteen, I thought that the freedom of adulthood and going off to college would be a new beginning for me. I believed that the sky wasn't a limit, and I was going to work hard to grab galaxies. However, there was one major issue within myself that I was unaware of. I thought that my drive for success and willingness to work hard was all I needed to become a successful, independent professional, but I was wrong. The problem with being wrong wasn't the mistake itself, it was living with the belief that I could become a happy, healthy adult without healing the traumatized child that still existed within me. Living with this unawareness has caused me to live a life of high hopes, followed by disappointment, anxiety, and depression. Being able to live my life as an eccedentesiast allowed me to appear happy and "normal" while in the presence of others but live as a depressed recluse at any other time. It took many years, but I realized that in order to live a life filled with joy and success, I needed to do things differently. I understood that I had to stop my one-woman pity party, and I decided to take control of my life.

First on the agenda was discovering me. I needed to develop an understanding of why and how I became the person who I am today. I knew this personal journey would be a long uncomfortable adventure, but I became dedicated to loving myself in a way that was unfamiliar and uncomfortable. This meant sitting and taking a nonjudgmental inventory of my attitude, actions, and feelings. After a lifetime of longing for approval from others and thirteen years on a job that caged in my talents and extinguished my passion, I knew that, as a person, I was in shambles.

While on my mission to find me and before I built up the courage to see a therapist, I completed many self-help surveys, and I stumbled upon one that asked the question, "What animal do you believe bests represents your personality?" I instantly began to think of the most powerful, clever, and independent animals that have roamed earth. Instinctively, I thought of an eagle. Eagles are independent, strong, confident, and clever. Everything that I believed myself to be. However, as time went on, I started to have a change of heart. I started to feel like the animal that represents me had to be one that is known to go be strong in the face of adversity, one that can go through a fire but emerge anew. Giving that question more thought, I started to remember the stories from Greek mythology, and I remembered the story about the phoenix. A phoenix is a mythological creature said to resemble an eagle. Myth has it that this creature lives for as long as five hundred years and that as it nears the end of its life, it builds a nest of aromatic spices, settles in, and sets it ablaze. While the fire burns, the phoenix relents to its fate and is consumed by the flames. As the embers cool, from the ashes emerges a new phoenix, who will knowingly succumb to the same fate. There wasn't a doubt in my mind that this animal, albeit fiction, is the animal that represents me! The story of the phoenix varies, but I admire how it lives its life helping others while remaining true to itself, and at the end of each phase of life, it prepares to enter a fire. The fire doesn't happen by chance, and the phoenix doesn't wait for the fire to appear. Instead, it builds a nest, and with a single clap of its wings, the nest ignites. The phoenix knows that in order to start anew, it *must* go through a fire. This seemingly unassuming question in a self-help article made me think of life in a much different way. I wondered how my life would begin to look if I truly lived with the mindset of a phoenix. If I navigate through life expecting fires to happen, I can learn to find peace in the flames and rise from the ashes.

I wrote this book in hopes of helping people everywhere find their inner phoenix. This is for the person who feels that God has more in store for them, but they do not know where to start. This book is for the person who wants to break the generational curses that have plagued their family for centuries. I hope that you join me on this journey. A journey where we will learn to control the flames of our lives, cool the embers that linger, and rise from the ashes.

My Fire
(1989–2008)

I believe that fire(s) can ignite at any moment throughout our lives. Unlike a phoenix, who ignites its own fire, our fires can be caused by circumstances that are out of our control. We will encounter many fires throughout our lives, but when the fire within us burns brighter than the fires around us, this is when we will learn to control the flames.

Chapter 1
Born in Fire

I was born a premature baby in June of 1985 in Miami, Florida, and just like many of the other children in my neighborhood, I was the child of an addict. Crack cocaine got ahold of my mom and has yet to let her go. I have flashes of memories from as early as three years old, and I remember living with her and my brothers, but I also remember spending a lot of time with my grandmother. I can remember our apartment in Opa-Locka. I can remember when my uncle would watch us for Mama and him, almost always, nearly burning the apartment down. My uncle was also an addict. His drug of choice was alcohol, and it gave him a knack for sleeping while cooking. When he would watch us, I knew that sooner or later there would be smoke engulfing the apartment. Someway, we always caught the fire before it was out of control, so this just became a normal occurrence. But I also remember that he was funny and playful, and more importantly, I remember that I loved him dearly. So when he died from cirrhosis of the liver, I remember being very sad. I remember when he became sick and was in and out of the hospital until the doctors told my grandma that there wasn't anything else that they could do to help him. With those words, my grandmother brought him home, and as she prayed and begged God to help him, she watched him die. When he died, I remember that I missed him very much. Although I was around three or four, I knew that I didn't just miss him with my head; I knew that I missed him with my heart. But in my family, we never mourned for long, so we went on like nothing happened and only spoke of him briefly from time to time.

Besides my memories as a toddler of my uncle, I remember having a lot of fun with my mom as well. As small children, my brothers and I had no idea that she was an addict. As a matter-of-fact, when my family talks about her during that time, they all agree that she was a fantastic mother.

I remember that I loved when she would play on the playground with us. The merry-go-round was my favorite, and I remember Mama spinning it until it was just fast enough for me to be terrified. Then, just as I thought that it would spin out of control, she would jump on with me and my fear would disappear. I remember when she would sit us all down on the floor to eat (she cooked a lot), and when the moon appeared in the night sky, she would call for us to come inside after we spent the day outside playing.

We lived in an apartment complex surrounded by family, so we were constantly being watched. My great- grandmother lived in a building in front of ours. Her brother also lived in our apartment complex, and we had a lot of cousins living in various buildings around us so, we were never alone. To add to the family who lived in our complex, my mom was the tenth of eleven children, and I always had an aunt, uncle, or cousin nearby. Although I was only about four years old, I remember enjoying the fact that I had such a large family. At that time, I didn't know what it felt like to be lonely. But very early in life, I realized that nothing remained the same, and little did I know that I would not only learn what lonely felt like, but it would dwell in my heart for a very long time. Eventually, those happy times with my mom were replaced with uncertainty and many depressing days. I don't quite remember what happened when my three brothers and I were separated and my mama lost our home, but I remember riding a jitney to my grandma's house and never returning to the home and family that brought me so much comfort and happiness.

For a long time, I hoped and wished that my mom would come and get me. I've always loved my grandma; but everyone knew that she was, for lack of a better term, *mean*. My grandma Ruby was a known hellraiser who spoke her mind (using words that would make a sailor blush). Standing around five feet three and weighing roughly one hundred pounds, she was known to be petite but mighty. She willingly and nonchalantly made more enemies than friends, and overall, she didn't trust people. When I went to live with her, I didn't understand what was happening, and no one said anything to me about moving. I was uprooted, and I had to deal with it. After the separation, my mom's visits were few and far between, but anytime she came around, I savored every minute and would become her shadow. I remember on one occasion, my mom, aunt, and grandma were having an argument; and even though I was about four or five, I knew what they were arguing about. My grandma and aunt were always getting on my mom about getting her life together and getting all of her kids back. Although I can't recollect exactly what was said, I remember hearing my mama proclaim that even if she won a million dollars, she would never come for us. She said that we were fine where we were, and it would do us more harm than good if she "uprooted" us. When I realized what she meant, I remember being incredibly heartbroken. I loved my mama and my brothers and wanted to go *home* with them. In my five-year-old brain, I thought this meant that I didn't have brothers anymore and that made me extremely scared. At five years old, I felt alone. No mama, no brothers, no *me*!

As time went on, I got used to living with my grandma and I tried to acclimate myself to my new *normal*. The times when I would go outside and play with my brothers were a distant memory. The fun times with my mom were rare, and although when she came around, she would take me outside to play, I didn't feel the same happiness that I felt when we were under the same roof. The happiness that I once felt when spending time with her was replaced by dread. I knew that our time together would be short lived and eventually she would tell me that she was going to the store and she wouldn't return for a few months or years. Even though I was happy to see her when she did come around, it was hard for me to find joy in those moments when my heart was so broken. I didn't understand why my love for her wasn't enough for her to change and regain custody of me and my brothers, but I had to deal with it and keep living.

Transitioning from a full-time daughter to a full-time granddaughter was difficult. I had to go from a child who ran with the boys, got dirty, and stayed out all day playing to a child who was seen and not heard (which was tough for me because I liked to talk). The most challenging thing to get used to was going from being one of four (and eventually six) to being just one. My grandmother did her best with me, and even though I was young, I recognized the sacrifice. I knew that we didn't have much money and that we lived in the projects, but it didn't bother me (almost everyone I knew lived in the projects). My grandmother did what she had to do to make sure I was clothed, fed, and provided for. Early on, I remember my grandmother being loving and generous. She would buy me toys and books, and I when I was scared at night (I was always afraid of being taken), she let me sleep in her bed. Although she was petite and didn't eat much, she was constantly cooking, and she made sure that I ate. Grandma didn't drive either, so we walked and caught the bus everywhere. To be in her late sixties, she was always on the run. I went everywhere with her, and I enjoyed it. Running around Miami meant that I wasn't bored in the house, and it also meant that I could sit and listen to my grandma and her friends reminisce about the good ol' days. During my first few years of living with my grandma, I quickly learned that when grown people were talking, I needed to look like I wasn't listening. In addition, I better not participate in the conversation of adults (not unless I wanted to taste my teeth) and do not interrupt them for anything if it isn't an emergency. I also learned to use *sir* and *ma'am* after my statements, and I was taught the number one rule of the house, which was to *never* tell anyone what was happening in our house. I was trained well on how to be respectful and polite, and in return, I was able to gain more wisdom than people ten times my age.

Although I liked hanging with my grandmother, I was still the only child in the house, which made me very lonely. That is, until my little brother was placed in foster care. I am not sure what happened, and how he got there. Rumor was, my mom left him with a family friend, and this family friend would lock him in closets, and I heard that he was even burned with an iron. Eventually, this family friend placed him in custody of the state. My youngest aunt felt guilty that he was the only one of my mother's children in state custody, and she wanted to get him out. My grandmother made it well known that she would *never* take in any of my brothers. It was said that when I was born, my grandmother told my mom that if anything ever happened and she lost custody of any of us, being the only girl, she would only take me. Even though my brother was in foster care, my grandmother stood by her word. My youngest aunt, on the other hand, couldn't let that happen; and she eventually went and got him.

My little brother Jatik came to live with us permanently; and, to be honest, I was scared. I couldn't remember how to be a sister anymore and didn't know how we would get along, but I was tired of being an only child, so I knew him coming was better than being alone. I hoped that he and I could create our own happiness although I knew that he missed my mama too. Jatik was the last of us to live with our mom, and his wounds were the freshest. I could see how much he wanted to be with her, and he acted out as a result. Jatik was a handful, to say the least, and anytime any of the adults in the family talked about him, they would include the fact that he was a "bad ass" little boy. But I didn't care about what anyone said about him because he was *my* brother and I was going to always make sure he was okay. Jatik's arrival also brought the attention of social workers. My grandma *hated* having social workers at our house. She cussed out each and every one that knocked on the door. Because my brother's adoption wasn't final, social workers had to come and talk to him and write a report on our family. Jatik, being new to the house, didn't know the number one rule: what happens in our house *stays* in our house. I remember one day we were all home, and my baby cousin was there. I was playing with her and allowing her to flip backward from my lap. Me, being around six or seven, I accidentally dropped her mid flip and her head hit the bottom railing of the bed. My cousin shrieked, and in ran the cavalry. My youngest aunt was really upset, and she proceeded to fuss at me. I have always been the type of person who would talk back or mumble something under my breath, so when she fussed at me, I sassed back. Out of frustration and anger, she threw a clothes hanger at me, and it hit me on my forehead and a lump the size of a quarter formed. Now once my grandma saw the lump, she said a few colorful words to my youngest aunt, which made my aunt leave for work in a hurry. That same day, my brother had a visit from a social worker. During their talk, my brother told the social worker that my aunt hit me with a hanger and put a knot on my head. Well, with obvious aspirations of making a difference with her clients, she came to our door and demanded to speak with me. The way she said it made me think that she looked at my grandma's size and underestimated her aggressiveness. She had no idea that the petite five-foot-three woman who was one hundred pounds soaking wet was a monster and didn't shy away from confrontation.

My grandma refused to let her talk to me privately, so with my grandma standing there, the woman looked at me and asked, "Sweetie, did your aunt hit you on the head?" I looked at my grandmother, and although I knew the golden rule of the house, I whispered, "Yes." Welp, it went downhill from there! The social worker sprinted out of the door, and in what seemed like seconds, there were policemen everywhere, along with someone who drove a rusty brown station wagon (which was the hallmark sign that children were being taken from families). They had come to take me and my brother into custody. I remember the policemen saying that everything would be okay and that I needed to grab a few articles of clothing and get in the car with the social worker. I knew that my grandmother would lose her freedom before she let them take me, but I didn't want to be separated from my brother again, so I remember grabbing a few pieces of clothing, placing them in a plastic shopping bag, and heading toward the station wagon. As my brother and I sat in the car, I could hear my grandmother arguing with everyone. My grandmother cussed them and called them everything but a child of God. Listening to her, my brother and I giggled because they didn't know what they were up against. Then I heard her yell, "If you are taking her, then you are taking me too." Suddenly, in comes my grandmother telling me and my brother to scoot over, and even though they were trying to convince her to get out of the car, she refused. "If they taking you, then they are taking me too," she said as she planted herself next to me. By this time, everyone in the projects were out watching the show. Somehow, my aunt was told of the commotion, and she returned home. She was greeted by the police and HRS personnel. I turned around and immediately felt uneasy. I had broken the golden rule of our house, and if I didn't go to the group home with my brother, I didn't know what would happen. Long story short, we weren't taken that day. I don't remember if we even got into trouble. However, I remember telling my brother that he had to stop telling the social worker everything that was going on in our house because I didn't want them to take him and I become an only child again. We both entered a pact that we would always stay together and that we would protect that with our lives.

By the time I was around seven or eight, I was much more aware of my circumstances, and although I found reasons to smile, I still could not shake feeling lonely, sad, and increasingly angry. But a change was coming. My cousin surprised my grandmother and bought her a house in North Miami. I was excited to move, although my grandmother didn't seem so happy. In my mind, we would *all* be moving and my brother and I would have a backyard to play in. But reality was, it was just me and my grandma who were moving. I was going to be an only child again, and that…hurt.

*****

6

I was almost eight years old when my grandma and I moved into a three-bedroom, two-bathroom home. It had a screened-in back porch and a large backyard. We also had a front yard where my grandmother had placed a gardenia bush. I thought that living there meant the beginning to a better life experience. My elementary school was about three blocks away, and the neighborhood was filled with kids. I wanted so bad to make friends and be able to have someone to play with. Jatik now lived on the opposite side of Miami, and it would take a long walk and a bus ride to see him. We rarely ventured back into Wynwood, so I only saw him when my aunt would bring him over. For about a year, I missed him terribly, and it was another hard adjustment. I started to feel like anyone who I loved would eventually be taken away, and I remember telling myself that I needed to become accustomed to it happening. When Jatik did come over, I enjoyed every minute of it, but for whatever reason, my grandmother would always make it seem like he was a burden. Nevertheless, we were happy to see each other, and that overshadowed anything negative. When he wasn't there, it would just be and my grandmother and the occasional guest or visiting family member. My oldest aunt didn't live far, so she would come over quite a bit to help us get groceries and run errands. Our new neighborhood wasn't near many bus routes, so we would have to walk long distances to get to where we needed to go. Initially, I didn't mind how much we walked or relied on public transportation, but after a while it became quite a chore.

We stayed in that house for about three years, and as I got older, it seemed like the good times faded. I found myself wishing on every shooting star, making the same wish when blowing out every imaginary birthday candle, and asking Santa for the same gift every year. I wished I could go home with my mom. I wished that she wasn't an addict anymore, and I wished I could have my brothers back. My mom's addiction was her number one priority, and although I would still feel happy about seeing her, it was not the same. When I saw Mama, I wasn't happy about spending time with her. I was just happy to know that she was alive. Anytime Mama would come around, my grandmother became uneasy. Being an addict means feeding that addiction, and if that meant stealing, then Mama would steal. I remember my grandmother hiding her valuables throughout the house. There were a few occasions when my mom was in the thralls of her addiction, and she stole from my grandmother. To hide her jewelry, my grandma would wrap it in aluminum foil and place in under the stove. Grandma didn't believe in banks, so she had cash stashed in various hiding places around the house. When my mom would show up, my grandma would wrap the money in an old stocking and pin it to her bra. But it didn't matter where anything was hidden, my mom would find it. I remember a few times when we had to visit local pawnshops searching from my grandmother's jewelry. A lot of the jewelry belonged to various family members who had passed away, including my grandmother's own children and her mother. So, when we weren't able to recover all of it, I knew that it broke my grandmother's heart. Even though I was young, I remember wondering why my mom would do this to her own mother. I knew that my grandma was mean, but she had a heart, and having her child steal from her broke it little by little. My grandmother was born in 1923 and had her share of pain. By the time I came along, I believed that she took some of that pain out on me. I knew she was hurting, and she had been for years, but my grandmother wasn't the victim type, and she didn't give anyone an opportunity to wrong her more than once. So Mama was *not* allowed in the house if my grandmother wasn't home.

When Mama did make an appearance, she would sleep for days, and once she was rested, off she went. My grandmother made it clear to Mama that she could not use our house as her "personal fueling station." When we left the house, Mama had to leave too. If I was home alone and Mama showed up to the front door, I was under strict orders to *not* open the door. I remember on one occasion when my grandma was out running errands and I had gotten home from school before she had gotten back home. While there alone, my mom showed up. I was about nine years old, and although I knew the rule, I loved my mom, so I let her in. Mama wasn't there very long before my grandma returned home, and she was livid! My grandma told my mom that she had to leave, and she obliged. Once my mom was gone, I was yelled at, but that was it, and I thought it was over. Well, a couple of days later my grandma realized that money was stolen along with some jewelry that was hidden in the house. She was frantic because the money was supposed to be used to pay a bill. At first, she accused me of taking it, but that theory evolved into me *helping* my mom steal it. My grandmother was furious at the thought of me helping my mom steal from her. I had received many a whopping from my grandmother before, but this was different. Convinced that I helped my mom steal from her, she felt betrayed, and I became an enemy. My grandmother, enraged, began to beat me with the handle of a wooden broom. We never owned plastic brooms, we owned the straw brooms with the thick wooden handles, and they hurt. After a few blows, I began to run from her. Although she was older and petite, she was strong and quick. Once the broom broke, she got a belt that belonged to my uncle and came after me, striking me with the buckle. I was in so much pain. I screamed in anguish, but no one came to my aid. Running from her, I remember tripping over something and falling to the ground. She then grabbed me by the ankles and tried to pull me back toward her in order to have me back within striking distance. I yelled again, "Someone help me! She's trying to kill me." After a few more strikes with the buckle of the belt, I guess she was tired and told me to go to my room. My body was on fire, and my heart was in shambles. From a very young age, I developed a relationship with God, and up until this point, I truly believed that He loved me and would protect me. I remember crying hysterically and asking God to please take me away from this life. Whatever that looked like…so be it. I knew that even if I went to school the next day, no one would notice the bruises, welts, or scratches. I was dark skinned, and nothing showed on me the same way as a lighter-skinned person. I have always been heavyset, and to look at my grandmother, she didn't look like she could inflict that much damage on a person my size, so who would believe me anyway. I asked God to please tell me what I had done that was so bad to deserve this life. My mom had chosen the streets over me, and now my grandmother didn't like me anymore. I was alone and sad, and I was a burden to everyone, so why did I exist?

During this period of time, school was my happy place. I didn't know I was smart, but I knew that anything involving word acquisition and vocabulary came easy to me, and people seemed impressed by that. I wasn't a straight A student. As a matter-of-fact, I learned early that I didn't have to try hard in class. I noticed that my teachers gave the most attention to the struggling students or the students who were behavior problems, so I played into that narrative. Even more, I desired attention, and I knew that people took one look at my grandmother and pitied me. I learned how to play off their pity and get the attention that I wanted. I inherited my grandmother's way with words; and me being an avid reader, sarcasm and wit became my second language. To top it off, I was a silly child at heart and having to be so guarded at home meant that school was my only outlet. So I was not performing to my fullest potential, had a smart mouth, *and* was a bit of a class clown. Needless to say, I made each of my teachers *earn* their paycheck. Eventually, they started sending me to the office. Some of them felt bad for sending me to the principal, but in order to be able to teach, they didn't have much of a choice. Thank God for my assistant principal, Mrs. Nolan. She became my elementary school mom. She found it odd that when they asked my teachers to send me with the work that I would be missing, I had already finished it. So anytime I was sent to the office (which was often), she made me sit and read with her. She was impressed with how well I read and spoke and asked me if there were other things that I liked to do. I remember telling her "I like to sing."

Mrs. Nolan looked at me and asked if I would sing for her. With everyone in the office watching, I felt my stomach drop, but I decided to showcase my voice. I closed my eyes and began singing "Run to You" by Whitney Houston. I loved Whitney Houston, so it was only right that I sing a song by the greatest to ever do it. I didn't sing the entire song, but when I was done, I remember the women in the office staring at me. When they finally spoke, all I heard was, "All right now!" and "You better sing that song, girl!" It felt amazing to be celebrated! Mrs. Nolan told me something that, for the first time, made me feel like I wasn't a mistake. She said "Tarreka, you are special. If you work hard, you can become something amazing!" Up until that point, I thought I was destined for misery. I didn't know what she meant, but it felt good to finally *feel good*. I felt so good about myself that day, I strutted home with my head held high and my chest poking out. When I stepped in the house, I told my grandmother about me singing for the office staff and the assistant principal. Then I asked her if she would like to hear me sing. She replied, "Yeah. Let me hear it." Although my grandma mistreated me at times, I loved her dearly and wanted her to be proud of me. So I closed my eyes, found my inner Whitney Houston, and started singing.

"I know that when you look at me there's so much, that you just don't see. But if, you would only take the time I know in my heart you'd find..."

When I was done with the first verse, I stopped and opened my eyes. I looked at my grandma and waited for her response. She looked at me for a second and said, "I don't see where that's so hot. It was okay." My feelings were hurt. I thought I did better than okay. But I looked at her, and to keep tears from falling from my eyes, I muttered, "Okay," and proceeded to my room.

After that day with Mrs. Nolan, the principal, and teachers worked on a plan for me to keep busy while at school. I began singing in the school chorus (and became a soloist), I was trained to be a peer mediator (they thought that if I learned to help others resolve their problems, then I would learn to resolve mine), I became a member of the Future Educators of America (FEA), I became a classroom buddy and spent time in our deaf and hard-of-hearing class where I learned basic sign language and made friends, and I was a teacher assistant (I basically graded papers and filed them away). Mrs. Nolan saw worth in me and decided that keeping me busy was the key to helping me become a better student. What Mrs. Nolan didn't know is that she would help me unlock a part of me that I never knew existed. I realized that I added value to the world and that made me feel powerful (in my own little way).

During my fifth-grade year, I learned that we were moving again. My grandmother had enough of staying so far away from her old neighborhoods and she decided that we would move back to Wynwood. I was not excited to go back because being in that part of Miami scared me. It was constant noise, violence, drugs, and everything in between. We moved from our three-bedroom house into a studio apartment. It was like living in a refrigerator box. For the first couple of months, I slept on the terrazzo floor of our apartment and my grandma would sleep in an old rocking chair that we got from a thrift store. Once we moved into the efficiency (this is what we called a studio in Miami), it seemed like the little money that we did have was completely gone. There were many days when the water from the faucet was all there was to drink and had it not been for the low cost of dry lima beans, rice, and ham hocks (or smoked neckbones), we wouldn't have eaten. The one good thing about moving back to Wynwood was that I was closer to Jatik. Our apartment building was only separated from the projects by a fence. Even though I didn't want to be back in that neighborhood, it still felt like home because my brother and I were back together. Not in the same house but closer than we were before, and that made me happy.

The transition back to our old neighborhood was not an easy one for me. I knew many of the kids in my neighborhood, but I also knew that I had been gone for years, and I didn't have any friends. I begged my grandma and aunts to allow me stay home and not go to school. It worked until my grandma received a letter from the food stamp office requesting verification of my attendance in school. So after being able to sit home for about a month, I was enrolled at Booker T. Washington Middle School in Overtown. On my first day, I had to ride the school bus, and I remember being terrified. The kids cussed like little sailors, fought anyone who they wanted, and had *zero* respect for authority. I could tell that they didn't have a Ruby waiting for them at home. My grandmother was a disciplinarian, and if I was accused of anything at school, I was guilty until proven innocent. So I made it my business to ensure that I didn't do anything that would warrant a whopping or a verbal scolding (which at times was worse than the beating). When I got to Booker T., I quickly realized that I would either be a victim, or I would learn to fight. At first, I thought that if I sat in the back of the class and read a book, I would be overlooked. Boy, was I wrong! The teachers quickly realized that I was a good reader and would always call on me to read out loud. This made me a target to the other students. It didn't take long for me to be bullied. I was called Blacky or Fat Ass, and since we didn't have money for new clothes and shoes, I was relentlessly teased about that. There were kids who would take my backpack and empty everything out of it onto the street and steal anything that they found value in. After a couple of months of this, I couldn't take it and decided to fight back. I quickly learned that "When in Rome, do as the Romans," and I became a complete terror at school. I used my sarcasm and wit to make anyone who crossed me feel small. If the students were going to hate me, I would give them a reason to. Teachers were also fair game, and I made their jobs *hard*. I felt like none of them ever tried to help me, so they were a part of my problem too. During my sixth-grade year, I had been sent to the office with a referral so many times that the assistant principal, Mr. Grice, would just hold up fingers, indicating the number of days I had to sit in In School Suspension

(ISS). After the fourth or fifth referral, they were threatening to have my grandma come in and sit for a conference. What they didn't know was that I had already changed the emergency contact information, and I knew that they didn't have a working number or the correct address for me. So for the next two years, I was disrespectful and fought anyone who thought that I was "soft," and when I was given out of school suspension, I would ride the city bus or walk to a local library and read. I knew that if I was ever caught, my grandmother would try to beat the black off me, but that was the only time I could find peace, and it was better than being in school.

Between eleven and fourteen, my home life had its ups and downs. My grandmother was now in her seventies and becoming more and more frail. She was still mean as ever, but she didn't always have the strength to resort to violence. So she would spew venom with her words. The words started to hurt more than a whopping ever could, and I started to prefer being hit. Bruises and welts heal, but her words took residence in my head, and they were all I heard when I tried to do anything. As a result, I became very fearful of everything. But living in Miami meant that I could not show that fear to anyone. So I learned to talk tough, and if the time came, I had to fight without reservations or remorse. I also learned that everyone in the world had a reason to criticize me, but I could take that power from them if I criticized myself first. Entering my teenage years, I no longer remembered what true happiness felt like. Happiness had long been replaced with the feelings that come along with survival. I was just trying to survive childhood and living in the hood.

As years rolled by, the large family that I grew up with was shrinking. I remember that my cousin, my grandmother's nephew, was killed. We called him Ghost, and from what I remember, he was always smiling, and I also remember that my grandmother loved and prayed for him constantly. But her prayers couldn't save him. While at one of Miami's infamous strip clubs, he was shot in the face, close range, with a shotgun. I remember when my grandmother got the call. It was in the middle of the night, and knowing that I was up listening to her conversation, she looked at me and said, "Willie is gone." Her face was filled with sadness, and so was my heart. Even though Ghost and I were a generation apart, he was family. At the funeral, he was unrecognizable, and then I realized that having such a big family meant having many more opportunities to mourn. Somewhere in that time span, maybe before or after, my uncle Marvin suddenly died as well, and when we buried him, we buried a piece of my grandmother's heart. Uncle Marvin was another uncle that I loved very much. I grew up and always had him around. Because he was an adult living with autism (before we knew what autism was), he was with my grandmother and I quite a bit. So when he died, I was again very sad, but in my family, there wasn't much time for grief. I learned to bury the grief in the darkest corner of my heart and ignore it until it went away. I had to move on because survival was a day-to-day struggle, and we didn't have the luxury of active mourning. With each death, my grandmother was also becoming sadder and sadder. She had eleven children, and by the time I was twelve, she had lost three sons, one was estranged, and some of her children had become addicts. There were many nights I heard her crying, praying and talking to God. No one knew it, but my grandmother was heartbroken and in more internal pain than any of us could understand. Even as a child, I wished that I could take her pain away. I thought that if she was happier, she would lighten up on me and I would be able to finally find some sort of peace.

My mom's visit during these years of my life were few and far between. But even still, I was happy to see her when she came around. There was once when I was about twelve years old, my grandma and I had gone to the washhouse (Laundromat), and she sent me back home to get more detergent. I despised the washhouse, so I took my time getting back. I decided to visit my brother at my aunt's house while I was out. My youngest aunt saw me walking and told me that my mom was at her house. I was so excited that I ran the rest of the way there. Imagine my surprise when I saw my mom bruised, head to toe with scratches, and her leg and arm were wrapped with bandages. I knew that my mom was known as a fighter on the streets, but this was not the result of a normal fight.

"What happened to you?" I asked.

"I had to jump out of a car" was her response.

She went on to tell me that she had been kidnapped and blindfolded and that she could tell by the way the men were talking that they planned to kill her when they were done with her. She said she knew she had to do something, so she managed to pry the car door open, and although she could tell that they were moving at a high rate of speed, she had to jump. Her jumping from that car saved her life. With all the death that plagued my family, I lived in constant fear that we would one day receive the call that my mom was the next casualty. Just the thought of her dying horrified me. As she told me the story, I wanted to cry. Not because of what she went through, but because I prayed for God to protect my mom and promised to help anyone I met if it meant He would help her. Her surviving this ordeal reaffirmed that He was listening. While she was healing, Mama was allowed to stay around for about two weeks. It was the longest amount of time that I spent with her since she lost custody of us. I was happy to have her around, but Jatik was the happiest of us all. He loved Mama with everything in him and dreamed of the day she would come and get us. Imagine his devastation when she felt better and told us that she was going to the store and didn't return. I knew she wouldn't come back, but I had to watch my brother stare out the window for days looking for her. The blanket that she slept with while she was there became his most valued possession. I hated seeing him so sad. I had learned to swallow my pain and disappear into my books, but he hadn't learned that survival skill yet. So he acted out in school and at home until finally my aunt decided to medicate him.

Mama eventually went to jail, and he didn't see her for over a year. He was always sad when my mama was incarcerated, but I liked when my mom was in jail. Depending on the facility, I knew how much time she had, and I knew that she was *safe*. I liked when she was placed in the Women's Detention Center that was across the street from my school. Normally, she would be serving a year and a day while she was there, so that meant an entire year of visits. Once I learned the process, I would visit her every weekday. I would sneak away from campus during visiting hours to see her. The correction officers felt bad for me, so they would let me visit even though they knew that I was supposed to be in school and technically I wasn't old enough to visit her alone. I had made a pact with an officer that when my report card came out, I would be allowed to continue my visits if I passed my core subjects. That was easy! I could make a C in my sleep at Booker T., so I never had any opposition when it came to visiting her. If there weren't many visitors after us, the correctional officers would even give us a few more minutes to talk when time was up. When our visits were over, I would go back to school, and one of my friends would sneakily open the front gate so that I could attend the rest of my classes and finish my day. I would never tell my brother about the visits because I didn't want him to become too excited and tell my aunt or grandma; but sometimes, to make him smile, I would tell him that mama stopped by and told me to tell him that she couldn't stay but she loved him. He always wanted to know why she didn't stay, and I would come up with some sort of lie, but knowing that she was okay brought him temporary solace.

After years of having only my grandmother as my parent, my father's family found me (after about four years of us being estranged) and began coming to get me on weekends and holidays. I was thirteen years old when my grandma allowed my father into her house to see me. When he walked through the door, I just stared at him. My brother was staying with us until my aunt got off from work, so I looked at him and asked him if he knew this strange man. The last time I had saw my father I was around nine years old, and I could not remember his face. My dad looked at me and said, "You know who I am?" I looked at him with a bewildered look and told him no. Once he revealed that he was my dad, I didn't know what to think. He went on to tell me that he and his family had been searching for me and that his sister would be picking me up the following day. I didn't know what to think or how to feel, but I looked forward to having a break. Now that I was a little older, I understood that although I wanted to leave my grandmother's house, she was elderly, frail, and an easy target; and I worried about her safety while home alone. But the next day, with a couple of grocery bags filled with clothes, I eagerly left to spend time with my father's family...and deep down inside I was beyond overjoyed because I finally had a chance to breathe.

Process Pause

Take the time to process what you have just read and reflect by answering the following questions:

What were your childhood aspirations? Why?

_____

_____

_____

_____

_____

What one word best describes your childhood? Why?

_____

_____

_____

_____

_____

How would you describe your parents/guardian? Why?

_____

_____

_____

_____

_____

As a child, what did you like or dislike most about your family?

_____

_____

_____

_____

_____

Chapter 2
Existing in Flames

By the time I was fourteen, my father and his family were a permanent fixture in my life. They made it a priority to never *lose* me again, and at this point in my life, they became the support system that I yearned for. I survived middle school and was ready to enter ninth grade and the new world of high school. In the fall of 1998, I was in a unique situation, and I had the opportunity to either stay at Booker T. Washington or attend Miami Jackson Sr. High. The issue was that Booker T. Washington was the first high school in Miami for African American students and was deemed a historical landmark. Our alumni fought and won the battle to have it returned to its original high school status. Although middle school at Booker T. was difficult, I looked forward to staying there for the next four years. My grandma and I were now living in Little Haiti, which was our fifth move in three years, and although I was catching two city buses to get to school, I was happy to have Booker T. as a constant in my life. When I turned fourteen, I felt different from the years prior, and I was much more comfortable at school than when I started as a sixth grader. I was much more confident in my abilities and talents, I didn't feel as guarded, and my referrals were few and far between. My grandmother was around seventy-five then, and although she still had a lot of spunk in her and her words could still bring a grown man to tears, she was aging, and it was showing. She was still petite, but I did notice that her cognitive function was declining. My grandma Ruby was normally very forgetful, but her forgetfulness was starting to look a lot like dementia. It was also around this time I noticed that when we would run errands and would cross the streets, I was no longer holding her hand for safety and guidance—she was holding mine! Even though my grandmother would still say and do things to me that hurt my feelings, I was becoming her silent caretaker, a heavy job for a teenager. My grandmother was a very proud woman, and she prided herself in being independent, so I had to look after her from a distance. She would hide the rent and bill money and forget where it was and accuse me of stealing it. She would also forget about the stove when she was cooking and would all but burn down the house. After a year or so of this behavior, I learned to watch her movements around the house without her realizing it, and in a roundabout way, I helped her figure things out and remember what she had forgotten. The only time I couldn't watch her was when I was in school. I remember on one occasion I arrived home and she wasn't there. I was only minimally alarmed because it wasn't out of the ordinary for her to run errands during the day. I didn't begin to really worry until around 8:00 p.m. We lived in a part of Miami where a very violent Haitian gang ran the streets. They called themselves Zoe Pound, and they were beyond dangerous. They were known to do home invasions, and there weren't any exceptions to who they would kill. Since my grandma Ruby was raised in Miami, she knew that our neighborhood was dangerous, and she seldom stayed out alone at night. So on this particular day, as the sun set over our apartment, I became worried. My youngest aunt didn't live far, so I called and explained what was happening, and she rushed over. As darkness filled the sky, she decided to call the police, and by the time they arrived, I remember going from worried to utterly terrified. I started to feel so guilty about her being alone. My mind was well trained to first think of the worst possible scenario, so by 9:00 p.m., anxiety and fear had consumed me. However, I was also well trained on how to keep emotions hidden, so although I was riddled with fear, I kept my outwardly composure. I recall, at some point that night, I went into the bathroom and dropped to my knees. My grandma would always say that when I needed God most, I could find him in a closet. I couldn't go into the closet without someone seeing me and thinking that I was losing my mind, so I went to the bathroom to look *normal*. In there I prayed with every fiber of my being that God was with my grandma and would bring her home. Even with how she treated me, she was all I had. It was around 11:00 p.m. when Grandma Ruby walked through the gate of the apartment complex. Although my grandmother was the family hellraiser, we all loved her and seeing her unharmed gave us permission to finally exhale. Of course, everyone was asking her what happened and why was she out so late. She told us that she had become confused and got lost when

19

trying to catch the bus home. This wasn't in any way normal because our apartment was at the intersection of Second Avenue and Seventy-Ninth Street, and the buses that she caught to run errands, both had stops that were a few feet from our doorstep. This hadn't ever happened before, but I was relieved that God heard my cry and brought her home, so I counted it all joy and knew that I would have to keep a closer eye on her.

Trying to keep an eye on my grandma was quite the challenge. She fussed at me about every little thing, and no matter how hard I tried to block her out, her words hit me like a freight train. Different family members were taking her to run errands, which meant that she was home more, and I didn't worry about her as much, so when I turned fifteen, I decided that I was over being bored and alone at home and I wanted to join a few extracurricular activities. I was now embracing the fact that I was different from most of the students at my school, and I wanted to join the clubs that suited me. So I joined the choral ensemble, school newspaper, yearbook, and I even became a flagette in the band. I worked hard in all my clubs and worked my way into leadership. I was very proud at how far I had come and the accomplishments I had made since first beginning at Booker T. As a matter of fact, my writing skills were acknowledged by our local newspaper, *The Miami Times*, and I was chosen as their "Teen of the Week." I also earned the opportunity to write articles for their "Teen Scene" section (which made me feel like a *real* writer). With all this experience, I signed up to write for my school's newspaper and yearbook club. I also went on to audition for the flag team (which meant being in the band). Coincidentally, all of the clubs were sponsored by a teacher named Mrs. Hammond, and we were not each other's cup of tea (at first), but she would play a pivotal part in my journey toward emotional healing.

Back at home, things were mundane and had become routine. Over time, my neighbors learned that my grandmother was impudent and would cuss you out for anything, so they tried to steer clear of her. We did have a couple neighbors who she liked, and she would hold friendly conversations with them from time to time. I remember one neighbor who exemplified compassion and kindness in a way that gave me permission to do the same. Her name was Miss Denelda, and she was the friendliest adult I had met at that point. My grandmother told Miss Denelda about my mom being an addict and how much of a struggle it was taking care of me. I hated listening to her talk about me to other people. It always seemed like she wanted them to believe that I was an awful granddaughter. But Miss Denelda didn't believe the worst about me. She felt sorry for me, and she went out of her way to try to make me smile. When my grandmother would scold me or just fuss at me for no apparent reason, Miss Denelda would call me to her porch and just talk to me about anything to take my mind off the situation. On occasions when she thought that my grandmother was being too harsh on me, she would defend me and tell my grandmother, "Miss Ruby, she is a good child. You shouldn't be so hard on her." My grandmother would still cuss up a storm, but she would stop fussing at me, at least for the moment. I remember once, on my sixteenth birthday, Miss Denelda knocked on our door, and when I opened it, she pulled me outside and handed me $100. I was stunned! She looked at me and said, "I wanted to make sure you received something on your birthday. I know times are hard, but you only turn sixteen once." I was shocked at such a kind gesture. To me, $100 was a lot of money to just give away. I looked at her and told her thank you, but I told her that I couldn't accept it from her. Even though I knew that we were impoverished, I was very prideful, and I didn't want anyone thinking that I needed them to do anything for me. Besides, for the past few years, my father, along with his mother and sister, would give me money or buy me something nice for my birthday. So I knew that my birthday would be celebrated at some point. It didn't matter how much I insisted, Miss Denelda would not take the money back. She told me that the money was between us, and I could use it however I wanted. Even though I wanted to keep it all to myself, my grandma and I were really struggling financially. With my grandmother hiding her money and food stamp card, then forgetting where it was and the bills piling up, we were using pennies to scrape by. So, even though I didn't have to tell her about the money, I did. At first, her pride told me to give it back, and I told her I tried but Miss Denelda refused to take it back. I thought that my grandmother would become offended, but she didn't. She went to Miss Denelda and thanked her for being so nice. I told my grandmother that she could keep the money, but she gave me $80 of the money and told me to keep it for my birthday. I took the remaining $80 and, while she wasn't looking, placed the money in her Bible right on top of the Ninety-First

Psalm. I knew that she read this scripture daily so, I knew that she would find it. Even though my grandma was, at times, my biggest tormentor, I loved her too much to only think of myself. I also knew that I wouldn't be there for at least three days, and I didn't want her in the house without money. My grandma Ruby read the Bible every day, and I knew that she would eventually find the four twenty-dollar bills that I placed in the book of Psalms.

While at my paternal grandmother's (Grandma Cat) house that weekend, I talked with my grandma Ruby and found out that she had indeed found the money. But with her mind starting to come and go, she thought she put it in the Bible. She told me that she was reading the Bible and drinking tea when she so happened to find the money. She attributed it to God not coming when we want Him but Him always being on time. I agreed with her, and I never told her that I placed the money in the Bible.

During this phase of life, I didn't see my mom much, and I had grown accustomed to it. I always knew that she would end up in jail eventually, so I would sporadically call the Women's Detention Center and ask if she was in custody. If too much time passed, I would become worried, and I would catch a bus to Opa-Locka and walk around looking for her. Sometimes I would find her, but if I didn't, I would ask people on the streets if they had recently seen her, and most of the time, they would tell me yes. That would put my mind at ease because it would let me know that she was alive and that was all I really needed to know. When mama did come around, our relationship wasn't the same. My grandmother didn't trust her, so she was only allowed to stay for a day or two, and anytime my grandmother left the house, Mama would have to leave too. When she was around, my mom would sleep for about two days straight, so it was like she wasn't there. Even my brother had gotten use to her not being in our lives, and he wasn't as bothered by her absence anymore. We were older, and we had finally internalized that our mother was an addict, and there wasn't anything that we could do about it. Realizing that we were on the doorstep of adulthood would make my mom talk a lot about how it was when we were toddlers. She started to tell us that if she had a house, she would get us all back, and we could live under one roof again. Even though I was around fifteen, I could still remember being a four-year-old and hearing her say that she would never come for us. Those words were attached to my soul, and they haunted me my entire childhood, so I knew better than buy into the fantasy of us being reunited. After years of my mom's disappearing acts, she was now a visitor in my life, so I didn't think much about her appearances anymore. My focus had shifted. I no longer prayed for my mom to regain custody of my me and my brothers. I was almost done being *raised*, and I was not the four-year-old that she remembered. I was nearly an adult, and thanks to being raised by my grandmother, my inner self was much wiser than my chronological age would have warranted, and I was wise enough to know that I wasn't my mother's daughter anymore. I was my grandmother's daughter. Everything about me was what Ruby raised, and I knew that even if my mom were to regain custody of us, it wouldn't be the same. So, instead of praying for our reunification, I prayed for God to place His angels around her and protect her. I accepted the fact that my mom was addicted to crack cocaine, and I knew that the only thing I could do is pray for her. Knowing that eighteen was a few years away, I knew that I needed to come up with a plan that would free me from my current situation. I spent a lot of time dreaming of a better life and praying that God would *give* me happiness. As far as my brothers were concerned, I realized that I didn't know them anymore. I only saw my oldest brother every five years or so; and I never saw the other three, besides Jatik, after our separation. I could no longer remember their faces! We were all familiar strangers to each other, and although I still loved them, I accepted that all I could do was pray that God kept them safe and hope that one day I would become *their sister* again.

Dimming

My grandma and I moved again, and this time, we were living in Allapatah. We lived closer to Miami Jackson Senior High School, but I refused to consider transferring. I was happy at Booker T. and even if that meant walking from Allapatah to Overtown, so be it. Our move was a smooth transition, but I was sad to be leaving Miss Denelda. She and I had formed a bond, and I was sad to be leaving her, but I promised her that I would stop by and visit as much as I could. To be honest, I had become numb to people leaving me, so I knew that I would get over it. Moving seemed to calm my grandmother down, but in the quiet, I continued to notice how much her cognition was declining. She was losing everything she put her hands on. There were times that she misplaced the keys to the house, money for the rent and bills, and everything in between. I knew something was wrong with her. I noticed that her eyes were dimming. She started to drastically slow down, and she seemed sadder and more confused than ever. Seeing as though I had spent most of my life trying to make her proud, I really wanted her to see me perform, but I knew that traveling at night scared her, so I relented to the fact that she may never see me on stage. She was aging, and my grandma Ruby was changing! Because she was still a hellraiser and knew how to run people out of our lives, my family didn't seem to notice. But I did. Even though she physically slowed down, she was still able to cut a person's soul with her words and she was still very much aggressive. Her aggressiveness coupled with her fading memory made it increasingly difficult for me to live with her as a teenager.

With her cognition declining, even though she knew that I was in extracurricular activities, my grandmother became convinced that I was a hanging out in the streets with random men when I was supposed to be at school practicing and that I was a thief and a liar. This was far from the truth, but it didn't stop her from treating me as such. During my teenage years, I spent my summers and many of my holidays with my father's side of the family, but the summer before my senior year, I had to stay home with my grandmother. I was not a fan of this plan, so I asked my father's girlfriend, who stayed in my neighborhood, if I could stay with her while I attended summer school. She agreed to let me stay with her and even extended her home to my brother as well. Although I stayed with my father's girlfriend, I would go back to check in on my grandmother daily, and I would still run errands for her and make sure that the house was locked up at night. One evening, after school, I went home to check on my grandma, but she refused to open the door. She was livid and was convinced that I had somehow gotten into the house earlier and stolen all her money. At the time, her check was only around seven hundred dollars, and she had misplaced all of it. This meant that we didn't have the rent money. Of course, it made it around the family, and my grandmother was able to convince my aunts and uncles that I had stolen the money. Her proof was the fact that I had a new dress and shoes that I wore to prom my junior year. I also had a new class ring, and was scheduled to participate in my senior trip to Orlando and Tampa. She questioned where I had gotten the money to do all of these activities and told everyone that I must have taken the money while at some point during one of my visits. What she didn't tell them about was the many conversations that we had where I explained that my a teacher, her family, my dad, and my paternal grandmother worked together to pay for everything. Nevertheless, I knew that I had to help recover the money, so I started trying to figure out what I could do for other people to earn the money, but before I could come up with a plan, my eldest aunt stepped in and made sure all the bills were paid. My eldest aunt knew that my grandmother was forgetful, and she was always there to help us. My grandmother eventually found the money hidden under the carpet in her room, but because she didn't announce it, many people still assumed that I had taken it. I knew that she felt bad for accusing me of stealing from her, so we both went on as it the incident never happened. To make up for the confusion, my grandma Ruby bought me new shoes for the upcoming school year. I was happy that I would have more than two pairs of shoes for school, so all was forgiven. That is, until one night after band camp. When I arrived home, my grandma was frantic and cussing about her youngest daughter coming to our house and "bothering things." I was confused because no one dared to touch my grandmother's things without her permission. However, upon closer inspection, I realized that she was upset about what was done to me. In my room, I discovered that my clothes were doused in shoe polish and the new shoes that my grandmother bought were all cut. To add insult to injury, the prom dress that I wore during my junior year was also slashed and covered in shoe polish. I was completely heartbroken. I couldn't wrap my mind around why anyone would destroy my things. I never had many material possessions, so I treasured the little I had. With tears in my eyes, I asked my grandmother why my aunt would do such a thing. Grandma Ruby told me that my aunt was still convinced that I had stolen my grandmother's money, so she made it a priority to destroy anything that she believed I bought using the money. I just didn't understand how I was born into a family with people who could do something like this to me. Up until that point, I always chose to believe the best about my family. I thought they were some of the most intelligent and clever people I had ever encountered. She didn't care that she destroyed all the clothes that I had to wear to school the next year. She didn't care that it was my senior year and that for the first time in years, I was excited to feel like a *normal* teenager. I was so hurt, and I didn't know what to do. I could tell that my grandma was also upset. She called my aunt and read her the riot act, but the fact remained that everything I had to begin my senior year with was destroyed.

Process Pause

Take the time to process what you have just read and reflect by answering the following questions:

What is the single most profound act of kindness toward you that you will never forget?

_____

_____

_____

_____

What's one word that describes your extended family (i.e., grandparents, aunts, uncles, cousins)? Why?

Example of Traits	
Positive	Negative
• Honest	• Nonchalant
• Generous	• Toxic
• Compassionate	• Cynical
• Affectionate	• Arrogant
• Dependable	• Dysfunctional
• Loving	• Estranged
• Thoughtful	• Tumultuous
• Loyal	• Strained
• Devoted	• Malicious

_____

_____

_____

_____

Fueling the Fire

Senior Year, 2003

My senior year was a pivotal point in my life. For the first time in many years, I felt alive. My usual feelings of sadness, fear, and loneliness were still there; but they were now living among enthusiasm, love, and optimism. I knew that I was destined for more than being known as the daughter of an addict. I realized that there was more to life than living in poverty, feeling like my existence was a mistake and constantly feeling like I didn't belong. It was this year that I stopped praying for God to save me, and I started praying for the wisdom and knowledge to save myself.

After my aunt destroyed my clothes, I had to figure out a way to replace them. So I called my dad and my grandma Cat. They told me that they would replace the clothes, but the caveat was that they could no longer pay for my flag team uniform and band fees. This put me in a bind because our flagette uniforms had to be ordered within a couple of weeks and without their help, I didn't have the money to pay for them. No uniforms meant that I wouldn't be able to march at Florida A&M University's and Bethune Cookman College's homecoming. This was simply not an option for me. I was desperate to do more with my life and visiting two of Florida's Historically Black Colleges and Universities (HBCU) would allow me to experience life on a college campus. I decided to tell my sponsor, Mrs. Hammond, what had happened to me. Without hesitation, she told me not to worry because she would ensure that my uniforms were paid for. Through fundraising, and some of her personal money, my uniforms were purchased. Mrs. Hammond didn't know it, but her simple act of kindness toward me restored my excitement about the new school year.

At home, it was much of the same. I couldn't seem to do anything right. It was like everyone was convinced that I wouldn't amount to much as an adult. For the life of me, I couldn't figure out what I had done that was so bad to make everyone look down on me the way they did. I even had a family member tell me that I was lazy and wouldn't amount to much more than working at a fast-food restaurant. I didn't see anything wrong with working at a fast-food restaurant, but she said it in such a disparaging way that I vowed to never work in a fast-food restaurant. At seventeen years old, I figured out that for me to find a life of happiness, I needed to be in the presence of happy people. I didn't know what it meant to have a positive mindset, so I set out to befriend people who radiated confidence, optimism, and resilience. Being on a journey of positivity, made it increasingly difficult to stay home and listen to my grandmother nag me about everything her mind convinced her was reality. Her cognition was still declining, but she still remembered how to take her anger out on me. On the brighter side, after years of being estranged, my grandma and her sister were speaking, and with them rebuilding their relationship, I could spend more time outside of the house. Since my great-aunt Myra was still driving, she and my grandmother would be gone for hours on the weekdays. This was good and bad for me because although I was able to spend more time focusing on myself, my grandma Ruby was still leery about what I was doing while away from home. I remember one evening, after band practice, I got home around 8:30 p.m., and I exhausted and looking forward to going to bed. My grandmother had long taken my key because she didn't want me making copies of it. So as I knocked on the door, she appeared in the window, shouting, "Go back to where you came from." She was convinced that I was gallivanting around Miami with some guy, engaging in *who knows what.* She refused to open the door and told me that I couldn't come in her house because she didn't *"house no hoes."* In that moment, I was tired physically, mentally, and emotionally. That night when she locked me out, as much as I loved her, she changed my heart. That night it dawned on me that I was sick and tired of being sick and tired. I knew that I was a good person, and I was tired of living my life under an invisible microscope that saw me through a muddied lens. I didn't have the energy to argue with her, so I left her house and stayed with my dad's girlfriend. The next day, I returned to my grandma Ruby's house, placed my belongings in a black garbage bag, and walked out of her front door into the unknown. I told her that I loved her and that I would be back to check in on her. I don't recall her saying much as I closed the door behind me, but I knew there wasn't any turning back. I could feel in my spirit that my life was about to change, I didn't know if it would be for the good, but I knew that I needed to find my own way.

I didn't have many places to stay, so I ended up at my grandma Cat's house, where I was welcomed with open arms. I knew that my grandma Cat didn't have a problem with me being at her house, but it didn't feel like *home*. Just as I did as a little girl, when my mother lost custody of me and my siblings, I felt homeless. I had always been a visitor in my grandma Cat's house, so to now consider it home was difficult. Luckily, I had become used to change so although I was feeling disheartened, I held my head high and went on as if I was fine.

Although I no longer lived with my grandma Ruby, I still went to her house throughout the week to make sure she was doing well. I would take her to run errands and look around the house and makes sure everything was safe and clean. My grandma always had a lot of frivolous junk in her house, and as her mental health declined, it was very important to help her keep the house as clean as possible. I loved my grandma Ruby, and despite our bad times, I felt blessed to have her and wanted her to know that I would always be there for her.

*****

It was finally time, and HBCU homecoming season had arrived! I was super excited about being in the parades and half-time shows of both schools. Visiting both schools gave me hope and made me excited for my future after high school. Each campus was full of students who looked like me, which made me feel like it was possible for me too. We were treated to the step shows, where we were able to see the Divine 9 (the nine historically Black Greek letter organizations that make up the Pan-Hellenic Council). The sororities and fraternities that make up the Divine 9 were nothing short of amazing on both campuses and seeing them made me eager to send my application to both schools. On our way back to Miami, I remember sitting next to Mrs. Hammond and telling her that I knew what I wanted to do after I graduated high school. Going to both schools was an amazing experience, but after visiting FAMU, I knew I had to return to the hill as a student!

Returning to Miami dragged me back into reality. My grandmother was still changing for the worst, and I didn't know how to fix it. I was terrified for her. I knew moving back to live with her would mean, once again, experiencing her constant verbal assaults; but she needed a caregiver. I started coming to her house more often and staying later to make sure the house was locked and secured before I left. She was much more forgetful by this time. She started forgetting if she ate, and she became very confused when she would leave the house. When I would take her to the washhouse (one we had been to many times before), she didn't recognize it. Being raised in Miami and never driving a car, she walked those streets countless times, but by this time, she no longer recognized them. She had dementia. I knew it, and I was heartbroken about it. Truth be told, I loved my grandma Ruby with my whole heart, and the last thing I wanted for her was to become ill. Here I was wanting to go off to college, but how could I leave her in the condition she was in? I could not catch a break! It felt like anytime happiness found me, sadness was nearby waiting to remind me of what my life was meant to be…hopeless. I watched my friends and the other teenagers around me have the luxury of being a child. They had the freedom to make mistakes, take life for granted, and take risks. Me, on the other hand, I was overwhelmed and was quietly falling into a state of depression. I started to believe that maybe I was destined for misery. Maybe I was created to suffer in silence, and it was silly of me to think that I could be anything more than the little four-year-old girl who yearned to be loved.

It became increasingly difficult to focus on school and the college-entry requirements, but Mrs. Hammond must have felt that something was wrong because she stayed on my case about my grades and fulfilling the requirements needed to be accepted into FAMU. I understood why she was being so hard on me, but with everything that was going on in my personal life, I still found it hard to focus. There were days that I wanted to disappear, but I kept trying to overcome the negative thoughts and feeling of despair. On the bus rides to my grandma Cat's house, I studied for the ACT and the SAT. I worked very closely with the CAP advisor, and I started working on my community service. I was very overwhelmed, but once I started, failure was not an option. I remember listening to my classmates talk about the schools they were already accepted into, and I felt like I was too late. At my school, there was a wall where they would display the students who were accepted to colleges and universities and their tentative majors, and I hadn't earned my spot on that wall. I felt so defeated, but I continued studying and working. On top of everything else, when the time came for my school to order diplomas, we found out that I was not on the list to receive one. Instead, I was slated to receive a certificate of completion. Being that I was one of a few students who passed all areas of the newly created Florida Comprehensive Assessment Test, on the first try, my school didn't realize that I had fulfilled that requirement. Thank God for Mrs. Hammond! She noticed the discrepancy and was able to rectify the issue. I had enough disappointment in my life at the time, and the last thing I needed was to receive a certificate of completion after graduation.

High School Graduation

June of 2003 had finally arrived, and graduation was upon me. I invited my mom, and she was supposed to come, but she didn't show. My eldest maternal aunt came in from South Carolina and made sure my grandma was at the graduation venue. My father and his family were also in attendance. I was so happy that day! When it was time to walk across the stage, I could hear my family screaming my name, and it brought tears to my eyes knowing that they were there to support me. Our graduation was one for the record books, and it marked the end of one chapter of my life and the beginning of another.

At the end of graduation, I hurried to the parking lot to find my grandma Ruby. Although I was excited to see everyone, I wanted to let her know that we did it, and I placed my medallion around her neck and gave her a kiss on the cheek. She was so proud! She looked at me and said, "You did good!" Hearing her say that meant everything to me. I was also able to tell her that I was accepted to Florida A&M University and would be leaving for college in the fall and that my tuition and room and board was covered by grants and scholarships. She smiled at me and gave me a hug. Growing up, my grandma Ruby never hugged me (or anyone else for that matter). So for the first time in my life, at the age of eighteen, I *felt* her love for me. At graduation, I could see that she had become even more frail. Everyone else thought it was just age, but I knew that my grandma was also beginning a new chapter of her life. I didn't know what this new chapter would entail, but I knew that the end of this chapter would mean the end of her. I wasn't ready to face that reality, so I buried it in the back on my mind and heart and went on with my life.

Process Pause

Take the time to process what you have just read and reflect by answering the following questions:

What childhood memory brings you the most joy? Why?

_____

_____

_____

_____

_____

_____

_____

What childhood memory makes you the most uncomfortable? Why?

_____

_____

_____

_____

_____

_____

_____

Chapter 3
Controlling the Flames

The Highest of Seven Hills

The time came for me to head off to FAMU. I was excited and weary all at the same time. Knowing that I needed support and assistance, Mrs. Hammond volunteered to drive me there and help me settle in. Before I left, I stopped to see my grandma Ruby. She was sad to see me go but told me to make sure I listened to my professors and did my best to come home with a degree. She didn't have much money, but she gave Mrs. Hammond around $40 for gas. When we pulled off, I sat quietly in the back, and as I watched my grandma Ruby's duplex disappear in the distance, I cried. It was weird because for most of my life, I looked forward to the day when I could leave her house and live life on my terms. But now that the day had come, my heart was so heavy. I felt incredibly guilty about leaving my grandmother, but I knew that to live a better life I had to leave. To alleviate the guilt, I vowed to travel from Tallahassee to Miami as much as I could to check on her and help as much as I could.

Although I was sad, arriving in Tallahassee was exciting. There were people from across the nation scattered about. Move-in day for freshmen was an event within itself, and it was chaotic to say the least. Thanks to my family, Mrs. Hammond, and her family and friends, I had just about everything I needed to start the year. I was going to be staying in McGuinn/Diamond Hall on the second floor. My roommate had already placed her things in the room by the time I had gotten there, but she had already left once I arrived. There were so many people in crammed in once place that I needed a break, and once I placed my things in my room, I asked Mrs. Hammond if we could leave for a while and come back. She always thought I was anti-social, so she obliged. We went grocery shopping and grabbed something to eat. Then once we returned to the dorms, Mrs.

Hammond told me that our time together was over. She could sense that I was nervous but told me that this would be my new beginning, and although I was scared, failure was not an option. She also gave me the number of some of her friends who still lived in Tallahassee and told me to call them if I really needed something or I needed to get away. I watched her pull off, and with five dollars in my pocket, I walked up to my dorm room and tried to hide my fear and became a student at Florida A&M University.

It didn't take long for me to make friends. The girls in my hall were very friendly, and unlike me, many of them were from families that attended and visited FAMU often. There were also a few of us from Booker T. who found each other. In high school, we weren't the best of friends, but in Tallahassee, we were familiar strangers, and we were each other's comfort zone. Going to classes was the highlight of my freshman year until I discovered party life on the Hill. Mrs. Hammond also had a friend in Tallahassee who had his own law firm. I called Mr. Parks, and he was like having a guardian angel in Tallahassee. Knowing my situation, he would check in on me to make sure that I wasn't going hungry and that I was adjusting well. On occasion, when his firm would go out for dinner, he would invite me to bring a friend and join him and the rest of the lawyers. What he didn't know was that I had a 5:30–8:00 p.m. class, and anytime he invited me, I would call one of my friends and walk out of class. At these dinners, I met his partner, Mr. Crump, and few of the other lawyers. They were all insanely intelligent and well versed. On one occasion, the firm was having a celebration, and Mr. Parks invited me to bring a few friends. My friends and I were apprehensive at first being in a room with so many successful lawyers, but we loosened up when they started playing spades. Spades was a game that I was good at, and given the opportunity, I would play and become my true self. This time, Mr. Crump was my partner. While we were playing, he started to talk about the road he took to become a lawyer. I could easily hear in his accent that he was a Southerner (a country Southerner), so I was intrigued. I thought for sure that for him to be as successful as he was, he must have had help. To my surprise, I learned that both he and Mr. Parks were raised by their grandmothers, and although they faced many challenges, their success was made possible because they worked hard for it. It was such a blessing to be able to sit and learn from such esteemed lawyers. Needless to say, because of my lack of focus on the game, we lost that game of spades, but the knowledge and motivation that I gained was worth the dime that was ran on us (a dime is when the opposing team wins ten of the thirteen "books" in the game).

It didn't take long for me to find my way in Tallahassee, but when I wasn't in class, I was checking in with my grandma Ruby. Listening to her on the phone worried me. Often, in the middle of our conversation, I would ask her if she remembered to check the doors and windows to make sure they were locked, and I could hear her call for me to come and check the windows and doors. She would forget that we were on the phone together, and she thought that I was still home with her. When she didn't get an answer, she would tell me to hold on, but she would never return to the phone. Many times, I would sit and listen to her fumble about, and I would try to yell for her, but eventually, I would just hang up. Sometimes I would call her back, but there would normally be a busy signal. Being a freshman in Tallahassee meant that I was over four hundred miles away from her and at least four years away from being able to become her caretaker. With so much time and space between us, all I could do is pray that God would keep her safe and provide for her, but that didn't stop me from worrying about her.

A few times per semester, once I received my net check from financial aid, I would buy a few Greyhound tickets to go home and help my grandma Ruby. I knew she would need help with laundry, cleaning the house, and buying groceries; so I felt compelled to come home as much as possible to help. While home, I noticed that her memory, although fading, was still intact enough for her to be the grandmother I knew; but it was diminished enough for me to notice behavior changes. She had begun to store any food that required refrigeration in the freezer, and there were also times when the refrigerator wouldn't be working at all. Each bus ride back to Tallahassee was emotional mainly because of how guilty I felt about leaving my grandmother to fend for herself. But I also realized that after losing my biological mom and becoming a full-time granddaughter, I felt in my heart that I was now losing the mother that raised me. The all-too-familiar feelings of sadness, disappointment, fear, and loneliness returned;

and I was no more ready for them at 18 than I was at four years old, but I had to graduate college, so returning home so soon wasn't an option. Eventually, I decided to reach out to my family for help. I called one of my maternal aunts, and after having her friend assess my grandmother's condition, my aunt went to Miami and took my grandma back to South Carolina with her. Once my grandma was with my eldest aunt, my soul breathed a sigh of relief. I thought that I would finally be able to focus on me, but as with everything else in my life, I was wrong.

As if attending college and watching my grandmother's mental and physical decline wasn't enough for a nineteen-year-old to manage, my brother Jatik had become homeless. He was sixteen years old and on his own. I wasn't sure what happened, but I knew that he was fending for himself on the streets of Miami. He was just a child, and the streets of Miami aren't what the magazines portray. Our neighborhoods were riddled with drugs, poverty, and violence. I worried about where he would sleep, what he would eat, and how he would provide for himself? Although we were the children of an addict, we had never touched drugs, and we vowed to always stay out of trouble. When I would talk to him from Tallahassee, I would ask him about where he was staying, and for a while, I learned that he was staying with my mom. Mama didn't have a place of her own, but finding out about him being homeless, she felt obligated to find them a place to stay. However, no matter where they stayed, it was always short lived. After months of house hopping, my mom could no longer find them places to stay, and with her still being an addict, consistency was a challenge. So my brother made the decision to go to the Department of Children and Families and become a ward of the state. I didn't know how we would keep in touch or what I could do to help. As a college student, I could barely buy groceries, but since I was over eighteen, I had to try to get custody of him. I tried looking for an apartment and getting a job, but with my course load, I became overwhelmed. I tried my best, but I had no choice. I had to let this situation play out. It was out of my control! Around this time, it seemed like I was coming unhinged.

In school, I knew what I was supposed to be focusing on, but I couldn't fight the constant urge to party. I knew that my future depended on me getting a degree; but being at a club, party, or at someone's house drinking and playing spades gave me a chance to just live in the moment. A chance to just be happy. Overindulging in those moments that brought me temporary happiness meant that I was starting to fail most of my classes. Any class that wasn't English, philosophy or public speaking was a definite F for me. Between not showing up for class and failing to turn in my assignments, I was classified a freshman two years in a row, and I barely had enough credits to be a sophomore in what should have been my junior year. My life was spiraling out of control. It was obvious that my grandma Ruby's condition wasn't going to improve, my brother was in a group home (again), I was drowning in course work, and my financial aid was going to run out in a couple of years whether I had a degree or not. Although I was motivated to succeed, it was so difficult for me to be more than the little girl from the projects. During this time of my life, I wanted to crawl into a hole and vanish. At FAMU, I felt like I was out of my league. I was so tired of being tired. I was becoming a shell of myself, but I couldn't let people see me fail, so I had to find a way to fake it until I made it.

Process Pause

Take the time to process what you have just read and reflect by answering the following questions:

Being an adult means something different to everyone, what does being an "adult" mean to you?

_____
_____
_____
_____
_____
_____
_____
_____
_____
_____

What is standing between you and your biggest goal?

_____
_____
_____
_____
_____
_____
_____
_____
_____
_____

When life becomes overwhelming, what do you do to take care of your mental and emotional well-being? List five things you do to alleviate stress:

1. _____
   _____

2. _____
   _____

3. _____
   _____

4. _____
   _____

5. _____
   _____

Draw It!

Many people are wearing a mask of happiness. Draw a picture of how you believe people perceive you and then draw a picture of how you truly feel daily.

My Mask	How I Actually Feel

Chapter 4
Burning and Destruction

There came a point when I started to watch my friends get closer and closer to graduation, and it seemed like I was never going to get a degree. By my third year, I had explored three majors: music education, journalism, and criminal justice. I was all over the place and really didn't know what I wanted to do. For someone blessed with so many talents, I couldn't focus on anything long enough to establish a major. I did, however, continue to check in on my grandmother. She had settled into life in South Carolina, and my aunt was doing an amazing job looking after her. My grandma still valued her independence, so my aunt got her an apartment in the same complex as my cousins and youngest aunt. Everyone participated in looking after her and making sure she was safe. She was officially diagnosed with late-stage Alzheimer's disease. I knew for years that she was suffering from dementia, but to hear it confirmed made it real. With this information, I felt like I needed to be by her side as much as possible. Every free moment I had, I found myself traveling to South Carolina to be by her side. Even when her disease caused her to become violent and aggressive, I still wanted to be by her side. I no longer feared my grandma Ruby. At this time in her life, I felt that she needed to feel loved and cared for, which meant that I needed to move past my fear of her and focus my attention on her well-being.

I remember one summer when I travelled to South Carolina and had a fun-filled Fourth of July with my grandma, cousins, and aunts. My grandma had me do her hair and pick out an outfit for her to wear to a cookout that my cousin was hosting. We had so much fun! Her memory would come and go; but on this particular day, even with her cussing us all out, our entire family embraced her walk down memory lane. We ate and laughed well into the night until everyone was tired of each other and departed from each other. The days that followed were, for the most part, uneventful. That is, until one Wednesday morning. I awoke that morning to water streaming from our ceiling. I immediately got up and went into my grandma Ruby's room to make sure she was okay. She was still sleeping, so I decided to let her sleep as I tried to figure out what has causing the leak. After about an hour, it was discovered that the person who lived upstairs had been out of town and somehow their sink had been left running and was overflowing. The maintenance manager turned off the water and wanted to bring us fans to help dry our apartment out. When I arrived back to our apartment, my grandma was still in the bed. I called for her, and she answered, but she still seemed very lethargic. It didn't seem normal, but I told myself that she was just aging and she needed more rest. As the day went on, I struggled to get my grandma out of bed. When I was finally able to get her out of bed, I washed her up and sat her at the table to eat. Her eyes seemed vacant, and although she was eating, I had to feed her. Up until then, I never had to feed my grandmother by hand. Something was definitely wrong! I called my eldest aunt and told her about the crazy day we were having. When I mentioned to her that I had to feed my grandma Ruby by hand, my aunt told me that she was on her way to our apartment. She also told me that it sounded like my grandmother had a stroke and that we needed to call 911. My heart sank. My aunt arrived at the apartment minutes before the ambulance. Once she talked to grandma, I saw tears begin to fall from her eyes. She helped me get Grandma dressed and ready to meet the paramedics, but I could tell that she was worried. I think in that moment we knew that the Ruby we all knew and loved was leaving us.

At the hospital, doctors confirmed that she had indeed had a stroke. They told us that it was evident that she had mini strokes before this one, and she would continue to have them after. While in the hospital, my grandma slept for what seemed like months. But I stayed by her side the entire time. I prayed and cried, day in and day out. I would leave her side only to find something to eat. Daily, my youngest aunt would come to the hospital early in the mornings and have me take her to work. She would tell me to take her car and leave the hospital for a few hours to take my mind off things. But I never did. I couldn't leave my grandma, even if she was just sleeping and didn't realize that I was there. I stayed and held my grandma's hand and read the Bible to her. I wanted her to know that she was never alone. The entire hospital staff knew my name, and I could tell that some of them felt bad for me. For weeks, I slept on a recliner next to my grandmother's bed, and every night before I closed my eyes, I begged God to bring her back to me. One night as my family sat around her hospital bed laughing and joking, my grandma Ruby opened her eyes and raised her head. Everyone was so engrossed in conversation that they didn't notice her at first, but she looked at my aunt and said, "Where we at?" When she found out that we were at the hospital visiting her, she became extremely confused. She kept asking, "Well, what is it? What did I have?" Finally, my cousin asked her to clarify what she was talking about. To which she replied, "The baby I had. Is it a boy or a girl?" The entire room erupted in laughter. My grandma was eighty years old, and she had given birth to eleven children over the course of twenty-five years. Besides giving birth, she rarely had to be admitted into a hospital. So she assumed that she was there because she had another baby. It was the funniest moment we shared as a family since the Fourth of July (a year prior), and for a moment, we had forgotten that the woman who was the matriarch and root to our family tree was sick and withering away. We forgot that she had Alzheimer's disease. We forgot to be sad! In that moment, the only thing we remembered was that we were family and as a family we loved Ruby.

The stroke affected my grandmother's entire left side. It caused her a lot of pain when we tried to stretch out her arm or stand her up, so doctors told us that she would have to go to a rehabilitation facility. Initially, I assumed that she would be there temporarily, but soon after her arrival to the nursing home, doctor's recommended that she stayed. At first, my family was totally against the idea of placing my grandmother, the matriarch of our family, in a nursing home. But after doctor's explained her condition and how she would need around the clock care, we knew we didn't have a choice. I, again, vowed to never leave her side. I wanted to be with her as much as possible to ensure that she wasn't being mistreated, but eventually, I had to get back to school. I received emails from my professors threatening to fail me, and I was struggling to maintain a 2.0, so I didn't have a choice. I headed back to the Hill.

Back in Tallahassee, I moved off campus and into a townhome with some friends (who happened to be male). Living and associating with girls was harder than I thought, and I felt more comfortable living with my male friends. Although I was sad to leave my grandma, I must admit that being back in Tallahassee was a needed distraction. Knowing that I would be facing academic probation if I failed any of my classes, I devised a plan to organize myself and earn better grades. It paid off, and I finished that semester on the dean's list. The following semester, I decided to drop a few classes so that I could spend more time in Miami and Charleston. At the beginning of the semester, when I got my net check, I went back to Miami to make sure my brother was well taken care of. Since he was moving from one group home to another, it was like searching for a needle in a haystack to find him. Some days I would spend the day catching different buses in hopes of eventually seeing him. Other days I would visit one of his old group homes and ask if anyone knew where he was. When I did find him, we would ride the bus to the flea market to get his hair cut, and I would use a portion of my net check to buy him any clothes that he needed. We would also visit different places and houses just to spend time with each other. Eventually, he would have to report back to the group home, and I would catch the bus alone, back to wherever I was staying at the time. When the semester ended and on holidays, I would be in South Carolina with my grandma. I knew our time was coming to an end, and I wanted to spend as much time with her as possible.

I continued this cycle of traveling from Tallahassee to Miami and to South Carolina for over a year. Everyone at my grandma Ruby's nursing home knew me and became accustomed to me staying all day with my grandma. In the nursing home, my grandma had good days and bad days. On her good days, I would take her outside and we would sit, talk, and listen to Shirley Caesar. On her bad days, we stayed inside and I read her the Bible and braided her hair. One night while we were talking, she began to cry. When I asked her why she was crying, she told me that she was sad because she would miss us. She told me how much she loved us and that, although she would be happy to see her mom and sons on the other side, she would still miss us. I cried because I knew she could sense that our time together was expiring.

Even though my childhood with my grandma wasn't the highlight of my life, I loved her with every ounce of me and couldn't imagine life without her. Overtime, her petite, frail body became weaker and weaker, and somehow, she contracted pneumonia. For a while, I thought that she would get better, but one day while in the hospital, I realized that she was tired. As she struggled to breathe, I remember kissing her cheek and laying my head next to hers. I asked her, "Mama, are you tired?" She stared out the hospital window and slowly nodded her head. I knew the time had come to say goodbye. Tears began streaming down my face, and taking a breath after each word, I whispered, "Thank you for taking care of me. Thank you for loving me. I am going to miss you! I love you so much." I put her hand to my face and wept. I was scheduled to go back to FAMU that same day, so my aunt took me to the train station immediately after leaving the hospital. I was able to hold my tears back just long enough to wave goodbye to my aunt from the train. As it pulled off, I whispered goodbye to my grandma and begged God to take care of her. I quietly cried all the way back to Tallahassee knowing that my time with my grandma Ruby was over. About three days later, I received the phone call that she was gone. I felt abandoned all over again. Now what was I supposed to do? What was the use in finishing school without my grandma being there to see it? I was sad and needed a break, so I took time off to grieve her death and help plan her funeral. A few months prior to my grandmother's passing, we also lost my uncle (her youngest son). As a family we were still mourning his death, and now my grandma was gone. It was a lot to process, but I had to continue to press on.

During my grandma Ruby's funeral, there was a light rain. There is an old saying that if it rains on the day of someone's burial, it is a sign that the person made it into heaven. Although it was a drizzle, it was rain nonetheless, so I took it as a sign that she just did make it in. There is also a saying that deaths in a family happens in threes, and my family proved this old adage to be true. My grandmother had a younger sister; and exactly four months after my grandma Ruby's death, her sister Myra died as well. The mood of my family was very solemn, and we were at the point where we just wanted the pain to go away. Personally, I was at a low point, and I didn't know how to save myself. Eventually, I would have to return to

FAMU and figure out how to graduate, but I was in survival mode and planning for my future wasn't at the forefront on my mind.

My grandma was buried in Miami, and I stayed there for a couple of months, house hopping from place to place, but Miami no longer felt like home. I felt like a stranger in my own city, so although I was born and raised in Miami, I knew that I had to leave and start a life of my own somewhere else. The more I tried to think about my future, the more I knew that I needed a degree to help me get a decent-paying job. So, I had to come up with a plan. The fires of my life seemed to be burning hotter than ever before. I needed to extinguish them…but how?

Process Pause

Take the time to process what you have just read and reflect by answering the following questions:

_____
_____
_____
_____
_____
_____

What emotional baggage have you taken from your childhood into your adulthood?

_____
_____
_____
_____
_____
_____

Word Association

After reading each word write the first thing that comes to your mind. Don't think, just write!

Happiness	Weakness	Mother

Discipline	Success	Love
Forgiveness	Family	Father
Failure	Home	Regret
Future	Sadness	Trust
Hate	Sacrifice	Destiny

Your Turn
The Fire

It is important to *Name Your Flames*. In this section, think about past situations and events that, when thinking about it, causes you to feel negative emotions. Did something happen to you as a child that still makes you sad, anxious, afraid, or angry? Maybe you endured a traumatic event that as an adult that still robs you of happiness. Suppressing the hurt and pain will not make it go away, but it will allow it to become a silent fire that will continue to burn unless you begin to extinguish it. Writing it down is the first step in controlling the flames that plague your life.

What are your flames?

Write your story:

_____

_____

_____

_____

_____

_____

_____

_____

_____

_____

_____

_____

_____

_____

Tarreka Garnett

Cooling the Embers

Overtime, every fire will start to decay. The decaying stage of a fire is characterized by a significant decrease in oxygen or fuel, putting an end to the flames. Time alone can help us begin to extinguish the fires in our lives. But while our fires are decaying, we have to be cognizant of the embers. Embers are the glowing fragments that serve as evidence that a fire is burning out, but if not cooled, the embers of our fires can be reignited. To completely cool the embers of our fires, we have to do the work. I believe that cooling the embers of our lives has to be done in three steps: Reflection and Responsibility, Education, and Planning and Execution.

Chapter 5
Extinguishing the Flames

I returned to Florida A&M University completely broken. I was grateful that, as a school, they rallied around me and tried to help me as much as possible. The semester that my grandmother died, I was granted a retroactive withdrawal, which saved my GPA, but it meant that I would have to take all five of those classes again. My friends also rallied around me and tried to help as much as they could, but being Ruby's daughter, I pretended to be fine and didn't accept any help. I couldn't risk anyone pitying me, so I wore a mask of happiness daily. I never had the luxury of mourning before, and now was no different.

I thought returning back to Tallahassee would help me find a sense of normalcy but being on the Hill didn't feel the same anymore. I didn't enjoy homecoming. I didn't want to attend my classes, and I just wanted to sleep the days away. I felt like everyone else was living their best life while I was struggling to greet the day. My grandma was gone, my brother was still in a group home and back in the system, and my mom was still an addict. I was trying to figure out my place in the world, and from my perspective, my life was a mess. But one day as I lay in bed, it dawned on me that I didn't have anything to fall back on. I had to move forward. I couldn't control what was happening around me, but I could control my response to those situations. As I spent most of my days fighting back tears and robotically going through the motions, I remembered my second year at FAMU. In my philosophy class, my professor showed the movie *The Secret*. I remembered how everyone in this movie talked about the law of attraction and how changing our perspective can change our reality. I remember looking at myself in the mirror, and it was then that I decided to cool the embers of my fire.

Step 1: Reflection and Responsibility

With nothing to lose, the first thing I felt I needed to do was take inventory of my life. I knew that my childhood was, for lack of a better term, traumatic; but I ignored how that trauma affected me as an adult. As a child, I taught myself to live in a fantasy world where I wasn't affected by how I was treated as a child. I became a master of moving on, but the residual effects of my childhood lived on in my personality and perspective. Here is what I learned about myself through my personal reflections:

What I internalized from childhood:

1. Happiness is short lived.
2. Having dark skin is a scarlet letter that will follow me for the rest of my life. The best way to cope with it is to shine through it.
3. Loneliness is inevitable, so embrace it and the peace that comes along with it.
4. Everything and everyone that I love will eventually disappear.
5. Nothing stays the same, so I can never become content.
6. I must always be on guard because anything could happen and anytime.
7. If I recognize my flaws first, I can't be hurt by others when they discover them.
8. I can't shy away from my intelligence because it is a major part of my survival, so I must always seek out knowledge and logic.
9. My brother is my responsibility, and I must make sure that he is cared for.
10. There isn't time in my life for sadness and grief, feel it for a second and move on.
11. Fear is an internal experience…keep a straight face and *never let people know when I'm afraid.*
12. The less people know about me the better.
13. Trust no one.
14. Protect myself *at all costs!*
15. Always think two steps ahead. This way I can't be caught off guard.

I also started to think about how I described and viewed myself. When I thought about words that defined me, I immediately thought of words like *kind, polite, creative, talented, well-spoken, driven, resourceful,* and *intelligent.* However, to truly cool the embers of my fires, I needed to also admit that I was defensive, angry, sad, anxious, irritable, closed off, difficult to work with, and a bit of a know-it-all.

While reflecting, I had to also confess that, although I didn't show it, I never healed from feeling abandoned by my mother; and because of this, I had a burning need to control all aspects of my life. I never wanted to feel like I did as a child. Growing up, I wasn't in control of my life, and because of that, I was forced to accept life as it came. To protect myself as an adult, if I am in any situation that feels uncomfortable, in the span of a millisecond, I will have flashes of several possible outcomes and imagine my reaction to each scenario. This type of thinking heightens my anxiety and places me in a fight-or-flight state of mind. But if I work to control the situations and events in my life, I can try to prepare myself for every outcome, which lessens my anxiety.

Thinking about my past and being honest with myself also forced me to admit that my inner voice was heavily influenced by my grandmother, and as a result, I was my biggest critic. I believed that there was something wrong with everything I did. When I shopped for clothes, all I could hear in my head was "Dark skinned girls can't wear this color." I was so hard on myself that, for the most part, I would avoid taking pictures. A picture was nothing more than a way for me to tear myself apart about how I look. In addition, anytime someone wanted to acknowledge me for any one of my talents, I would always nitpick myself and comeback with something negative. If someone said, "I like your necklace." My response would be, "Thank you. It was $10 so I know that it is going to turn green soon." I would say it in a joking manner, but it was just to cover up the fact that I didn't think that I was worthy of a compliment. The voice in my head was the most negative thing in my life as an adult, and *I couldn't turn it off,* although I wanted a better life, I didn't fully believe that I deserved it and I was subconsciously self sabotaging my chance at greatness.. I was a master at dreaming of better, but I didn't know how to be anything more than the smart, dark-skinned girl from Miami. Finally, in order to grow into the woman I wanted to be, I needed to acknowledge that I was still the little girl who yearned to be acknowledged and validated. I presented as an adult, but my younger self was the puppet master. My childhood experiences are what shaped my personality, and I needed to unlearn the thinking and behaviors that were in direct response to my trauma. Those thoughts and actions protected me as a child from the hurt and pain that I was enduring, but in order for me to evolve into the woman I wanted to be I needed to learn healthier behaviors that would benefit me in my future endeavors. As I deepened my reflection of self. I realized that there were a lot of fires that I created or fed. For example, I had been written up at work for being late (a few times). The reason why I was late was because I would wait for a friend of mine to pick me up and take me to work. I didn't like catching the city bus, so I knew I would be late, but I thought it was worth it. I could extinguish this fire by catching an earlier ride or simply riding the bus. Another fire that I could begin to extinguish was making sufficient time to complete my assignments and study for my classes. I was still catching the bus to Miami to make sure my brother was doing well, but I needed to start using that time to become a better student. I was also chronically fatigued and felt like I was walking around in a fog. I knew that I needed to see a doctor and take better care of myself so that I could be a healthier me. The more I reflected on myself, the more I realized that I had a lot to figure out.

Step 2: Education

After being open and honest with myself, I decided to educate myself more about the effects of childhood trauma. For years I convinced myself that I was fine, and that it was everyone else around me was the problem. I knew that I had to change this way of thinking so that I can begin to find joy within myself. I knew that if I could understand the effects of my childhood trauma on my adult life, I could finally reduce the heat of the flames in my life. The first thing I did was search the Internet for answers on childhood trauma and its effect on the brain and adult behaviors.

I kept a journal where I wrote down scientific evidence that helped to explain childhood trauma and its effects. Through my research, I learned that childhood trauma is the personal experience of a child that is emotionally painful or distressful. This experience (or experiences) often results in lasting mental and physical effects. I knew that my experiences from childhood had mental effects, but I sat and thought about any lasting physical effects that my childhood trauma could have had. I finally looked at myself in the mirror and realized that my weight was my physical effect. At this point, I was topping the scales at around two hundred pounds (standing at five feet four). For the majority of my life, I was heavy, but I remembered that I wasn't heavy prior to living with my grandma. As a teenager, I would starve myself to lose weight, but I gained it all back the longer I stayed at FAMU. My weight was the physical evidence of my childhood trauma. I also learned that what I had experienced as a child was called interpersonal trauma. In addition, I realized that being physically and emotionally abused, rarely hearing "I love you" from my grandmother, along with the constant berating and being separated from my mom and brothers all classified as traumatic experiences. For complete healing, I also had to consider that my grandmother had a lifetime of traumas that affected her and hindered her from being the best person she could have been.

After developing an understanding of what trauma is, I wanted to know how it affected my brain and behavior. I learned that my childhood trauma caused me to activate my fight-or-flight responses repeatedly. At home, I had to walk on eggshells every day in the hopes of not angering my grandmother. This day-in and day-out behavior took a toll on my brain's development, which caused the frequent release of adrenaline and cortisol. Now that I am an adult, it is possible that my brain has trouble regulating that process. This means that my fight or flight can be activated very easily, even in times when no threat is present. I also discovered that, as it relates to brain development, childhood trauma can adversely affect the amygdala (a part of the brain that has to do with processing fearful and threatening stimuli), prefrontal cortex (a part of the brain that has to do with focusing, predicting the consequences of ones actions, impulse control, and planning for the future) and the hippocampus (a part of the brain that has to do with learning and memory). A damaged amygdala can lead to increased anxiety and fearfulness in a traumatized child. A damaged prefrontal cortex can result in difficulty focusing, poor memory, and difficulty with critical thinking. And a damaged hippocampus can mean impaired memory and mood control. Personally, I struggled with constant anxiety and fearfulness as well as focusing on any one project or assignment for a sustained period of time. I also had very poor short-term memory, and my mood could change in the blink of an eye. Once I understood how my childhood trauma affected my brain development, I needed to know if and how I could be "fixed."

When researching ways to "fix" myself, I read many journals from reputable sources on mental health. Many of those articles stated that we must stop thinking that we can be "fixed." As a survivor of childhood trauma, I was still a whole person who needed to change my way of thinking and replace certain negative behaviors with healthier behaviors. These negative behaviors were coping mechanisms that no longer served me and were now getting in the way of my emotional and mental healing. I also learned that I needed to seek support from a professional, not isolate myself (which is something that I tend to do on a regular basis), and I also needed to be patient with my process and progress.

At Florida A&M University, I decided to take advantage of the counseling services on campus. As a woman of color, I knew that in the African American community seeking out and utilizing mental health services was a sign that I was mentally weak and frail. Just like other Black women, I was taught to suffer in silence and take my burdens to God. Although I had a relationship with God, I needed to talk to someone who could answer me out loud, so I made an appointment to see a counselor. My counselor was very nice and during our first meeting, I was very nervous. I wasn't comfortable with telling her everything because, in my mind, if I told her everything about me, she would have the ammunition she needed to belittle me in the future. During our first meeting, it was somewhat quiet. I completed a questionnaire, she read it, asked me a few questions, and I left. It was underwhelming to say the least, but I went back again. During our second visit, she asked me about my childhood. I nonchalantly told her that it was "okay." When she asked me to describe my good memories, I told her about the family gatherings of both my mother's and father's side of the family, visiting my aunt in South Carolina during the summers, and listening to my grandma talk about how life was for her as a child and as a young woman. She then asked me about the "not so good" memories. I hesitated, which created a long awkward silence, but after about a minute or two, I told her about my grandma raising me and that she had recently died. I also told her about how difficult my upbringing was. We talked briefly about my grandmother's death and how I was managing my emotions, and at the end of our second session, she told me she wanted me to work on identifying my feelings. She said that she felt that I needed to learn to feel different emotions, even if they are painful.

At my third session, she wasted no time asking me to list the emotions I felt because of my grandmother's death. I remember telling her that I was sad, lonely, and guilty; but I also felt relieved. Sad and lonely, she understood, but she wanted to know why I felt guilty and relieved. I told her that I watched my grandmother deteriorate for many years, and I cried many nights, feeling bad that her health was declining. Her dying meant that she didn't have to continue to decline and become a shell of herself. I was relieved that she was no longer suffering. I also felt very guilty about her death. I knew that there wasn't anything that could be done to prevent it, but when she had her initial stroke (that landed her in the hospital), I felt guilty for not being smart enough to recognize the signs of a stroke. After that stroke, I found out that if a person receives medical help within the first four hours of the stroke, the effects can be reversed. For years, I felt guilty for not doing sufficient research on Alzheimer's and for not knowing the signs of a stroke. I felt like her life could have been extended had I known. My therapist reassured me that my grandmother's death was not a result of my lack of knowledge. She let me know that everything I was feeling was a part of the grieving process and it was normal. In addition, through talking with my therapist, I was able to admit that I had slipped into depression. Toward the end of my third session, we talked about strategies that I could use to achieve small goals over a short period of time. She helped me to understand that setting goals and holding myself accountable for achieving those goals would help me overcome depression and ultimately graduate from FAMU. I was not enjoying Tallahassee anymore, so the idea of graduating was motivation enough to get me up and going. But with all that was going on, could I do it all?

Step 3: Planning and Execution

I was the queen of procrastination, so it took me over a month to finally draft a list of goals and develop a plan to achieve them. I purchased a dry-erase calendar from the bookstore, and I started by first writing my assignments and their due dates on the calendar along with my work schedule. Knowing that I tended to drop everything and attend a house party to drink and play spades, I decided to not attend anymore house parties for the remainder of the semester. I was proud of myself for setting goals, but it would be difficult for me to meet every deadline. The more I planned, the more I became bogged down with the details of the plan and would feel overwhelmed. When I brought this up to my therapist, she helped me work to consolidate some of my goals. This made my calendar look less intimidating and more feasible. She also suggested that I begin developing better study habits by committing to a few days a week for a couple of hours of day. Her suggestions helped me tremendously. As soon as I arrived home after her session, I made it a priority to plan out my day. I made sure that in the course of a week the majority of my days were very similar. I believed doing the same thing every day would help me develop better habits.

In addition to having a calendar and writing down a plan to achieve my goals, I began thinking about a movie I saw that talked about the law of attraction, and I made a vision board. I placed pictures of women graduating college, a car (I really despised catching the bus), a house, and a lot of happy people (just living). I put it on my wall as a pictorial reminder of what I was trying to accomplish. After making my vision board, I realized that after a while, the board became a part of the paint, so I started to move it to different places in my room. This forced me to look at it just about every day and helped to keep me focused. It took a few weeks, but I eventually learned how to strategically plan the achievement of my goals.

During this process, I realized that completing the plan was easier said than done. I was very impulsive and would find myself skipping due dates or skipping class altogether. At one of my therapy sessions, I remember feeling embarrassed when she asked me about how I was progressing. I admitted to her that I had been slacking off, and I think that she could see my anxiety begin to heighten. That's when she told me that I needed to work on becoming more disciplined and holding myself accountable. As we conversed, I realized that every accomplishment that I attained in life was motivated by proving me wanting to prove someone else wrong.

My aunt told me that I was lazy and would probably amount to nothing more than a fast-food worker, so I graduated and vowed to never work in fast food. My grandmother made me feel like everything that made me special was a curse, so I made it my business to be recognized for my talents in a positive way. Now that I was in college and on my own, I didn't know how to motivate myself. At the end of our session, she tasked me with finding ways to encourage myself and reminded me of why I needed to remain disciplined and stick to my plan. My financial aid would run out in a couple of years, and I needed to graduate with a degree. So I left her office, and although I didn't know what my life would look like in the future, I knew that I couldn't allow to look like it did in the past. That was motivation enough for me to keep going and figure it out as I went.

I worked diligently every day to stick to my plan, and I also remembered to be patient with the process. I was doing something that was never modeled to me, and essentially, I was building the plane as I flew it, but I knew that with discipline and continued self-encouragement, I could achieve whatever I put my mind to. By the end of the semester, I made the president's list (straight A's), lost ten pounds, and was approved for twenty-one credit hours during the summer. Learning how to set goals and strategically planning to achieve those goals were only part of what helped get on track. For my plan to be executed, I had to become disciplined (without excuses). Once I started to see the fruits of my labor, my next step was learning to celebrate my "*small*" successes.

Your Turn
Cooling the Embers

Reflection and Responsibility requires you to think deeply on past situations and take responsibility for the behaviors that you have developed as a result. Understanding that you can only control *your* thoughts and actions, what are some attitudes and behaviors you can modify that will benefit your future?

Reflective questions to consider:

- Who are you when no one is looking?
- What are you afraid of?
- What beliefs or behaviors do you have that no longer benefit your life?
- Is your childhood trauma still affecting your adult life? How?
- Are you being your authentic self in life?
- What can you change about yourself that will positively impact your life?
- Are you holding on to negative feelings that you need to let go of?
- What do you want most in life?
- Do you take care of yourself physically? Emotionally? Spiritually? Mentally?
- Are you using your time wisely? How do you use your time productively?
- What matters most in life?
- Do you speak more than you act?
- What makes you anxious? Fearful? Sad?
- What have been your biggest mistakes? What have you learned from them?
- How often do you think negative thoughts? What are the negative thoughts? How can you change negative thoughts to positive thoughts?

Reflection and Responsibility

Reflect and answer the following questions:
What words describe you best? Why?
Examples:

Positive	Negative
Joyful	Angry
Optimistic	Reclusive
Kind	Resentful
Resilient	Pessimistic
Proud	Controlling

_____

_____

_____

_____

_____

_____

_____

_____

_____

_____

_____

What are afraid of? How does that fear affect you?

_____

_____

_____

_____

_____

_____

_____

_____

_____

_____

Are you holding onto something (anger, resentment, guilt, etc.) that you need to let go off? If yes, explain.

_____

_____

_____

_____

_____

_____

_____

_____

_____

_____

What beliefs or behaviors do you have that no longer benefits you?

_____

_____

_____

_____

_____

_____
_____
_____
_____
_____
_____

What can you change about yourself that will positively impact your life?

_____
_____
_____
_____
_____
_____
_____
_____
_____

What do you want most in life?

_____
_____
_____
_____
_____
_____
_____
_____
_____
_____
_____

What do you do to take care of yourself?

Physically

_____
_____
_____
_____

Emotionally

_____
_____
_____
_____

Mentally

_____
_____
_____
_____

Spiritually

_____
_____
_____
_____

What have been your biggest mistakes? What have you learned from them?

_____
_____
_____
_____
_____
_____
_____

What are your negative thoughts?

What do you do when these thoughts arise?

_____

_____

_____

_____

_____

_____

_____

_____

_____

_____

_____

Use the following space to write any other reflections of yourself or your life:

_____

_____

_____

_____

_____

_____

_____

_____

_____

_____

_____

_____

_____

Education

Education is an integral part of self-healing. Stepping outside of your emotions to understand what science says about trauma and its effects on the human brain will help you discover strategies that are researched based and have been proven to be successful. If you are considering therapy, it is important to educate yourself on the different therapists in your area and as well as their style. Educating yourself will help you cool the embers of fires that are slowly extinguishing. Education can also be an integral part of preventing the heat from old embers from reigniting into flames.

Questions to consider:
- What is childhood trauma?
- What is psychological trauma?
- How does (childhood) trauma affect the brain?
- How does poverty affect the brain?
- What strategies can help me organize my life?
- What adult behaviors can be linked to childhood trauma?
- How can I overcome childhood/psychological trauma?
- What behaviors are a reflection of my childhood trauma?

Question	Answer
What is childhood trauma?	

Research the answers to the following questions:

Question	Answer
What is psychological trauma?	

Question	Answer
What effect does childhood trauma have on the brain?	

Question	Answer
What effect does poverty have on the brain??	

Question	Answer
What behaviors are linked to childhood trauma?	_____ _____ _____ _____ _____ _____

Question	Answer
What strategies can be used to overcome childhood trauma?	_____ _____ _____ _____ _____ _____

Use this page to write the answers to any lingering questions you want to research on:

Question:

_____

_____

_____

_____

Answer:

_____

_____

_____

_____

Question:

_____

_____

_____

_____

Answer:

_____

_____

_____

_____

Question:

_____

_____

_____

_____

Answer:

_____

_____

_____

_____

Tarreka Garnett

Question:

_____
_____
_____
_____

Answer:

_____
_____
_____
_____

Question:

_____
_____
_____
_____

Answer:

_____
_____
_____
_____

Question:

_____
_____
_____
_____

Answer:

_____
_____
_____
_____

Planning and Execution
Creating a SMART Goal

SMART is an acronym that helps you evaluate and organize your goals

S	M	A	R	T
Specific Your goal should be clear, simple, and specific. This will help you stay focused and motivated.	**Measurable** You must have a way to accurately measure the success of your goal. If you find it hard to measure the success of your goal, it may not be specific enough.	**Attainable** Your goal needs to be within your power to achieve. Ensure to give this section of your SMART goal a lot of thought. You can potentially foresee potential barriers and work to avoid or solve them.	**Realistic** You can't expect to become CEO of a company six months after being hired as a secretary. When you make unrealistic goals, you risk becoming overwhelmed and frustrated when you realize that all your hard work won't result in success.	**Timely** Every goal needs a timeline. Having a timeline creates a sense of urgency and will help you stay organized and focused. Make sure to include a starting date and a target date. Try to schedule checkpoints so that you can reflect on your progress and make any adjustments.

Remember that SMART goals can be written for every aspect of your life, from personal goals to professional goals. Make them all SMART.

SMART goal example (written in May of 2006):

Weak Goal: I will graduate with honors.

SMART Goal: By the end of December of 2008, I will increase my grade point average from 2.5 to 3.0 (or higher). I will do this by studying four to five times per week and turning in all assignments on time.

S	M	A	R	T
Increase grade point average from 2.5 to 3.0	Increase grade point average from 2.5 to 3.0	Studying 4-5 times per week and turning in all assignments on time	I will have a year and a half to attain this while taking between 5-7 classes.	Target date for success: End of December, 2008

Create your SMART Goal

Goal: _____
_____
_____
_____

Using the information from your goal, complete the boxes.

S	
M	
A	
R	
T	

Check-in dates:
- _____
- _____
- _____
- _____

Create your SMART Goal

Goal: _____
_____
_____
_____

Using the information from your goal, complete the boxes.

S	_____ _____ _____
M	_____ _____ _____
A	_____ _____ _____
R	_____ _____ _____
T	_____ _____ _____

Check-in dates:

- _____
- _____
- _____
- _____

Create your SMART Goal

Goal: _____

_____

_____

_____

Using the information from your goal, complete the boxes.

S	_____
M	_____
A	_____
R	_____
T	_____

Check-in dates:

- _____
- _____
- _____
- _____

Create your SMART Goal

Goal: _____

_____

_____

_____

Using the information from your goal, complete the boxes.

S	
M	
A	
R	
T	

Check-in dates:

- _____
- _____
- _____
- _____

Rising from the Ashes

To most people, ashes signify the conclusion of an event or situation. When a fire burns out, what remains are the ashes of what was there before the flames. I, on the other hand, think of the presence of ashes as an opportunity to rise anew. Just as the mighty phoenix is reborn in the ashes, I too think of the ashes of my fires as my chance to show who I have become. The ashes are evidence that I have lost and learned, and they give me permission to emerge as a better version of myself. It's time we embrace our ashes. They are our evidence of redemption and proof that we have done the work to heal and learn from our past fires.

Chapter 6

Removing the Soot

The summer of 2006 was hot, and I was swamped with assignments from school and working over thirty hours per week. Even though there were times when I was overwhelmed, I remained disciplined and stuck with my plan. I finally declared my major and was on my way to graduating with a Bachelor of Science in elementary education. To graduate on time, I needed to take twenty-one credit hours every semester (including the summer) for the remainder of my time at FAMU, and I also had to take and pass the Florida Teacher Certification Exam. Since it took me three years to declare my major, I was very behind, and to accomplish this goal, I had to remain focused. So I became a recluse. Many of my friends didn't understand this, and in my quest, I neglected to tell them my plan. Soon, I stopped hearing from many of them. When I did call, they wouldn't answer or our time together seemed awkward, so I got the message and accepted that our friendships had come to an end. It bothered me for a while because I thought we would be lifelong friends, but I had a lifetime of loss, so I moved on without thinking twice about it.

Even though I had a lot going on in Tallahassee, I still found time to travel to Miami to check in on my brother and mom. My mom seemed to be attempting to do better and that made me feel hopeful. I knew that addiction was a disease and that she would struggle with it for the rest of her life but seeing her try made me feel like there was a chance she could beat it. My brother was still in a group home, but he had adjusted and was just waiting to turn eighteen. Keeping in touch with him was difficult, but regardless of where he was placed, I always found him, and I would make sure that he had everything he needed. Being in a group home meant that there was hardly ever enough to go around, so when I would buy him stuff, the other boys would steal it from him. It was frustrating, to say the least, but I would always take him shopping and hope for the best.

At this time, I was around twenty-one years old, and through persistent searching, I had located all my brothers (my mother's children). I had always known where my older brother, Jatik, and one of my younger brothers was; but there were two who lost touch with my family. My baby brother, who I hadn't seen since he was a toddler, was top priority for me to find. The story was that in the nineties, he was being taken care of by a friend of my mother. This woman loved my baby brother as her own, but she was disabled and in a wheelchair. One day, after we were all separated, everyone stopped hearing from her. When someone went to check on her and my brother, they found her dead with my brother near her body. From there her mother took my brother, and they relocated to another city. No one saw him since that day. My family tried to find him, but it was to no avail. But one day while I was on Myspace, I started my search. At that time, social media was a new concept, and young people everywhere were exploring it. My search was long, but once I figured out that we didn't have the same last name and with the progression of social media, I found him. Looking at his profile picture I knew it was him because he looked a lot like my other brothers. I reached out to him and shared what I knew of him and his story. He was apprehensive at first, but after seeing pictures of our other brothers he let down his guard and became excited to meet everyone. I also had another brother who was only ten months younger than me who had moved away from Miami. He lived with his paternal grandmother in Ft. Pierce, Florida, and although we saw each other sporadically as children, we lost touch as teenagers. To find him, I had to get help from my cousins in Miami. They were able to send a message through his father, and we reconnected as adults. For the first time in my life, I knew the whereabouts of all five of my brothers. When we were all separated, there were only four of us living with my mom and Jatik was an infant. I had no memory of ever living with my two youngest brothers, but I did remember seeing them as babies. Finding them all felt good, but we were strangers to one another with our own separate lives and experiences. I loved them all, but besides Jatik and my older brother, I didn't know any of them, so I proceeded with caution.

My life as a young adult was starting to look promising. I was starting to come into my own, and I felt better prepared for life. I felt like the embers in my life were finally cooling, and I needed to begin showing off my newfound self. When I started at Florida A&M University, I was walking around with a mask of happiness covering the brokenness of my soul. Now I was more confident, educated about myself, and motivated to begin creating the life that I yearned for. Around the age of twenty-one, my perspective of life had drastically changed, and although I was still battling the negative self-talk and doubts, I actively implemented strategies that helped me become more mature, self-confident, and self-reliant. As a young adult, I understood that everything I wanted in life (including happiness) I would be responsible for creating. I was finally on a quest to living a joyous and fulfilling life, and I knew that to find these things, I needed to change my environment and the people around me. So I began to associate myself with individuals who helped me see the good in myself. When people would say positive things about me, I would ask them to explicitly tell me why I deserved those affirmations. That question made some people uncomfortable at first, but because I was taught to believe that something was inherently wrong with me, I needed them to help me see myself in a different way. In this phase of my life, I realized that women who were older, more mature, and more experienced in life didn't mind answering my question. Many other African American women experienced similar trauma, and they were well versed in healing, so the more I listened to those women (and even some men), the more I was able to add to my self-healing toolbox.

Keeping it closer to home, I began to converse with my eldest aunt more with the intent of listening to her talk about life lessons she learned over the years. I also would talk to my grandma Cat and her sisters and listened intently as they talked about learning to set boundaries and not feeling obligated to explain those boundaries to other people. My eldest aunt taught me about scheduling quiet time with God. She would tell me about taking time out to talk with God and freeing my mind of clutter so that I could hear Him. I also continued to talk with Mrs. Hammond, and with her being a FAMU alumnae and growing up in the inner city of Miami, she was able to teach me how to "code switch" and assimilate myself to a professional environment. Coincidently enough, when speaking to the older, more mature women in my life, they were repeating things that were said when I was a child. I realized that the work I had done to become emotionally and mentally healthier caused me to now be able to receive these messages. Because I no longer thought, behaved, and spoke as a child, I wasn't as defensive, so I was able to listen and internalize what they were saying to me. I was becoming a new person and doing the work to unlearn habits and behaviors from childhood was tough but feeling like a whole person, made it well worth it. With me preparing for graduation, I was finally ready to show how much I had grown as a student, professional, and, most importantly, as a person. After five years, I was leaving FAMU with less fires burning in my life, the embers of past flames cooling (and some extinguished), and after working to remove the soot of past traumas, I was ready to rise from the ashes.

Process Pause

Take the time to process what you have just read and reflect by answering the following questions:

List five things, about your wellness journey, that you are proud of.

1. _____
   _____
2. _____
   _____
3. _____
   _____
4. _____
   _____
5. _____
   _____

List five changes that you have made or that you plan to make to improve your emotional and mental well-being.

1. _____
   _____
2. _____
   _____
3. _____
   _____
4. _____
   _____
5. _____
   _____

Chapter 7
Emerging Anew

The closer I got to graduation, the more "official" I felt. I officially felt like I could create the life I yearned for. I officially let go of everything that hurt me as a child and focused my time and energy on accomplishing the goals I set for myself. I was ready to emerge anew, but the question was, how? How do I show the world who I had become? Pondering on this, I realized that showing the world shouldn't be a priority. What others thought of me was the least of my worries. I spent most of my life worrying about what someone else thought of me, and it hadn't gotten me anywhere. The work I did to begin to heal mentally and emotionally wasn't for anyone to acknowledge, it was for me to become a better version of myself. I needed to prove to myself that I had changed. The only way to rise from my ashes was to succeed. Accomplishing my goals would inherently place me in situations where I would have to be a different person. I knew that emerging from my ashes would be tricky, but I was finally a senior, and with graduation around the corner, it was time. With me interning, my trips to Miami were few and far between. As Jatik neared eighteen, I knew he would age out of his group home, and I would be able to bring him to me to visit. My mom was still trying to kick her addiction. She was still in the thralls of it, but she seemed to have started to search for help. I realized that I would not be able to save her from her addiction, so I prayed and left her in God's hands.

In the spring of 2008, I was twenty-two and in my senior year at FAMU. I was a member of the gospel choir and worked thirty to thirty-five hours a week at a deli. For three straight semesters, I took twenty-one credit hours (seven classes) and was able to bring my GPA up to a 3.7, which was a drastic change from the 2.6 I had in my second year. I had also passed the general knowledge and professional portions of the Florida Teacher

Certification Exam, and after graduation, I would officially become a teacher. I was also continuing to create SMART goals for myself and organize my life so that I didn't feel overwhelmed. I remember the moment when I reflected on my time at FAMU and realizing how much I had changed and matured. I also had a boyfriend who made my happiness his main priority. At first, it felt strange having someone who was focused on my happiness. The voice in my head wanted me to believe that he had an ulterior motive because no one would ever be that nice to me without wanting something in return. But because of what I learned in therapy, I was able to overcome the negative self-talk and begin building a relationship with him. I had accomplished so much, but my biggest accomplishment was realizing that my journey to happiness and healing would take a lifetime. I had spent my entire life waiting for a better life to find me, but at this point, I knew that the happiness I was looking for was inside me.

Graduation

I had spent five years of my life on the Hill, and it was finally time for me to say goodbye. Being a student at FAMU was one of the best things I could have done for myself. I went from an eighteen-year-old who, for lack of a better term, was a mess to a twenty-three-year-old woman who accepted that I was a perfect imperfection. I was ready to leave Tallahassee and embark on the next chapter of my life, and this time I was in total control!

The week of graduation was hectic, but I was excited to have made it to the finish line. The days leading up to graduation were filled with packing and preparing to leave Tallahassee. My boyfriend had come up from Tampa to help me pack and move my belongings. Having him there to help me was such a blessing because I knew that I would be overwhelmed trying to do everything myself. Being the first to graduate from college, I had a slew of family who came to celebrate with me. My mom, brother (Jatik), Dad, Grandma Cat, and my aunt Margo had come up from Miami. In addition, my eldest aunt, my cousin, and Mrs. Hammond and her family were also there. There were moments that I wished my grandma Ruby was there to see me, but I was grateful to have so many other people there to celebrate my accomplishment. The work that I did to better myself emotional well-being made it possible for me to live in the moment and feel the love that was surrounding me. My anxiety was still heightened with all the attention I was receiving, but I didn't let my anxiety overtake me and blind me to the beauty of the moment.

It was April 29, 2008, and graduation day had finally arrived. At the graduation venue, I met up with some friends for Miami that I attended high school with. We were so proud of each other. Being products of the inner city, we weren't expected to make it this far. Many of our classmates had lost their lives while we were children, so we felt blessed to have made it have made it to that point. Before the ceremony began, we had to complete some final paperwork, and there was a dress code compliance check. I didn't have the money to purchase anything new, but I made do with what I had, and it was good enough. While we waited for the ceremony to start, I noticed that there was a table for students who were graduating with honors and needed their honors cords. It was a goal of mine to graduate with honors, but I wasn't sure if I was able to do so considering the abysmal start to my college career. I wanted to ask the woman at the table to check the list for my name, but I was afraid of the embarrassment and disappointment that I would feel if I wasn't on the list. So I decided to protect my happiness and graduate like a normal student. Our ceremony was beautiful! As I walked out, I could hear my family screaming my name, with my mom front and center. My heart swelled with so much pride and joy. Up until this point, I couldn't remember a time when my mom was in attendance to celebrate anything with me. The little girl in me was overjoyed to have her there, but the woman I had become recognized that it was my grandma Ruby who was owed the appreciation of this moment. By this time, I had reconciled the hurt of my childhood and knew that my grandmother's sacrifices were her way of showing how much she loved me. As a traumatized child, it was impossible for me to see life beyond what was physically in front of me. But as a woman on a journey of healing, I knew to find hope and happiness through my own trauma was growth but learning to love and appreciate my grandma Ruby through her lifetime of trauma was true healing. Just as my childhood trauma caused me to behave a certain way, so did hers. Once I learned to see my childhood through my grandmother's eyes, I was able to acknowledge the good in her and forgive the bad. That forgiveness gave me the freedom to love unconditionally, which allowed me to love my grandma Ruby for herself and appreciate everything she had done to help me get to this point. So I knew that I couldn't appreciate this moment without appreciating her.

Our commencement speaker was Bishop Eddie Long, and he was nothing short of amazing. He gave a captivating speech, encouraging us graduates to continue to work hard and make a difference in our communities. I'm not sure how my classmates felt, but when he concluded his speech, I was inspired. The ceremony lasted for what seemed like forever, but when it had reached its end, I walked across the stage as an official alumna of Florida A&M University. I had done it! I was the first in my family to earn a college degree, and I was very proud of myself. After turning my tassel, I met my family outside the venue and took pictures. I was having a graduation party at my mentor's law firm later that day and still needed to prepare for it, so after talking with everyone and taking pictures, I had to leave.

Later at the law firm, my family, friends, and coworkers were there to congratulate me. This was the first time that I had ever thrown a party for myself, so I was very nervous about making sure everyone had a good time. In time, my anxiety subsided when I noticed that everyone was enjoying themselves. Everyone talked, played spades, and had an amazing time. At the end of the night, although I was exhausted, I was overwhelmed by how loved and supported I felt. When I returned to my room, I remember falling to my knees and thanking God for always being with and taking care of me. There were some students who came to FAMU, and because of many different reasons, they left the Hill worse off than when they came. I, on the other hand, was leaving the Hill a graduate and a better person than when I arrived. Before I went to sleep that night, I recall going through my mail and opening a copy of my official transcripts. A professor I had told me that I should order a copy of my transcripts, so I was clear on what prospective graduate schools and employers would see about my time at FAMU. Once I read through them, I saw that at the end it stated my final GPA. After spending five years in college, having lost my grandma Ruby, and going through so much, I had come back from having a 2.1 GPA my sophomore year to graduating with a 3.2 GPA. This meant that I had indeed graduated with honors. That night, as I lay in bed, all I could do is think about how excited I was to move on with my life. I had decided that I didn't want to return to Miami, so I was going to Tampa to become an elementary school teacher. I was moving in with my boyfriend, and I was ready to start my new life in Hillsborough County.

Process Pause

Take the time to process what you have just read and reflect by answering the following questions:

Where do you see yourself five years from now?

_____

_____

_____

_____

_____

_____

_____

_____

_____

List five things you hope to have accomplished in the next three years.

1. _____

2. _____

3. _____

4. _____

5. _____

Chapter 8

Rising from the Ashes

As the embers of my childhood flames cooled, it was time for me to rise from the ashes. Truth be told, I had become comfortable existing in my ashes. Ashes are what's left when something has burned, and I was proud of what I was able to burn. In the short span of five years, I was able to burn my fear of not being enough and the fear of rejection and abandonment that haunted me well into my adult years. But best of all, I was able to burn the wall that was chained around my heart and replace it with a wall that was easier for others to penetrate. Being in my ashes shielded me from any other fires that had the potential of starting, and those ashes had become my safe space, and I was able to reacquaint myself with my greatness. But as comfortable as my ashes had become, I knew to be a true phoenix, I needed to rise from the ashes, spread my wings, and soar to new heights. So now that I had graduated and moved to a new city, I prepared for my resurgence. To successfully emerge, I knew that I needed to be strategic. Getting to this point was a long arduous journey, and I had to be cognizant of any behaviors that could sabotage my progress. At this period in my life, I found myself reflecting on the story of the phoenix. I had always found it admirable how, at the time of rebirth, the new phoenix knew nothing about the life ahead of it; yet it still emerged smarter, stronger, and more powerful than it was at the end of the last level of its life. To embody the spirit of a phoenix, I had to have the courage to do the same.

To be proactive in my preparations for rebirth, the first thing I did was develop nonnegotiable standards for my life. Having these standards would help me remember my values and principles and give me a foundation to build on as I adjust to the *new me*. I decided on five rules, and as time and life went on, I would add or subtract as needed. My rules:

1. I will consult God before I act.

2. I will not compromise my boundaries for anyone.
3. I will never allow anyone to insult, belittle, discourage, or demotivate me.
4. I will protect my mental peace and health at all costs.
5. I will work to bring the best version of myself to all my relationships.

Developing these rules, albeit just five, took weeks; but I felt a sense of comfort once they were written out. I also made it a point to develop a medical history of myself. Growing up, I didn't have a pediatrician, and outside of a couple of emergency room visits, I never visited a doctor's office. Now that I was an adult, I wanted to know what was physically going on with me so that I remain healthy. I knew that the school district that I would be working in offered full medical benefits, so I made it a priority to start seeing a doctor and a therapist as soon as I could. To continue to prepare myself for emergence, I also worked on my negative self-talk. Being raised in a household where I was made to believe that I was less than and that my talents were something to be ashamed of, my inner voice had become my loudest critic. To combat this, I researched ways to think more positively about myself. This is when I learned about self-affirmations. Self-affirmations are the act of affirming one's own worthiness and value to increase one's confidence and self-esteem. Simply put, to battle the voice in my head, I had to speak positively about myself. With this information I created ten affirmations:

1. I am confident.
2. All I need to succeed is within me.
3. I am strong.
4. I am intelligent and focused.
5. I can achieve anything that I put my mind to.
6. I am independent and self-sufficient.
7. I am grateful for everything that I have been blessed with.
8. I am not defined by my past, but I am driven by my future.
9. I am an asset to this world .
10. What I have done today…is enough.

I wrote these affirmations on sticky notes and posted them on the wall of my room. Each day when I got out of bed, I would read each sticky note. and slowly, I started to believe the words that were written on them.

The final thing that I did to prepare to rise was I learned how to celebrate myself. The thought of celebrating myself made me uncomfortable, and up until this point, I thought of self-celebration to the trait of a selfish person. My entire life nothing was ever done to celebrate me. So now that I was a young adult, I didn't know how to celebrate myself. As a matter-of-fact, I never felt like there was anything in my life worth celebrating. However, now that I was on my journey of healing and rising from my ashes, I knew that it was important to learn to celebrate me. Celebrating myself, to me, meant taking time to acknowledge the positive things that I had done in my life and the successes I had achieved. Because this was a new way of thinking for me, I made of list of things about myself that I thought should be celebrated.

1. I am still here and working toward a better future.
2. I have learned to enjoy the journey toward emotional healing.
3. I have a college degree.
4. I am better today than I was five years ago.
5. I have learned to be thankful for the small things in life.
6. I have continued to develop my talents and skills.
7. I have learned to love me.
8. I am self-sufficient and self-motivated.

At first glance, my list seemed short, but I knew that as time went on, I would be able to add to it. So I made it a priority to find at least one thing each day that could be celebrated.

It's Time

After all my preparation, it was time. Slowly, I began to spread my wings, dust off the ashes, and rise. I didn't want to rush the process, so I took it day by day. Each day, I recited my nonnegotiable rules and affirmations, set goals for the day, and found something about myself to celebrate. Some days were tougher than others, but little by little I settled into my new level of life. By the end of the summer of 2008, I was employed as a fifth-grade teacher, and (because I had a cousin who also lived in Tampa) I was meeting new people who I would have previously shied away from. Things were going well, but I was in constant fear of something going wrong. But I reminded myself that I was entering a new level of life and I needed to take it slow and extend myself grace. I was starting to feel happiness again. Not momentary happiness. I was experiencing a happiness and joy that lived within me, and although it felt foreign, I was genuinely joyful with life. I felt more confident, outgoing, and in control of my life. As scared as I was to emerge from the comfort and *predictability* of the ashes of my past, I was glad that I made the decision to rise. This new level of life felt unfamiliar, but I felt like I belonged there. The happiness and joy that I felt didn't blind me to the fact that there would be new fires that I would have to fight, but it felt good to know that the old flames were behind me.

Process Pause

Take the time to process what you have just read and reflect by answering the following questions:

Nonnegotiable Rules/Standards

Create five to ten nonnegotiable rules/standards for your life. When creating your nonnegotiables, remember to be faithful to your desires and happiness.

1. _____

2. _____

3. _____

4. _____

5. _____

6. _____

7. _____

8. _____

9. _____

10. _____

Personal Affirmations

Create five to ten personal affirmations for your life. When creating your affirmations, remember to write the positive version of any negative thoughts you may have about yourself.

1. _____

2. _____

3. _____

4. _____

5. _____

6. _____

7. _____

8. _____

9. _____

10. _____

Celebrations

Take this time to celebrate your accomplishments. No accomplishment is too small, so write as many as you can.

1. _____
   _____
2. _____
   _____
3. _____
   _____
4. _____
   _____
5. _____
   _____

6. _____
   _____
7. _____
   _____
8. _____
   _____
9. _____
   _____
10. _____
   _____

Chapter 9
Spark!

Life was great! Being in a new city gave me a chance to become the woman that I imagined myself to be. Now that I was a fully free flying phoenix, I felt more in control of my new level of life. I didn't know how to work at anything below an elite level, so I quickly started to formulate a plan to take Tampa by storm. I didn't want to feel like the weakest link on my new campus, so I reached out to my friends from FAMU that had already began teaching for advice, and knowing that I would be a novice teacher, I began researching strategies and methods that would serve me in the classroom. I also made it a priority to meet women in the community who were women of purpose, and with my cousin's help, I found my way to the women of the Tampa Metropolitan chapter of Delta Sigma Theta, Sorority Incorporated (DST). While at FAMU, I always admired the women of DST, but because I was constantly traveling to Miami and South Carolina for one reason or another, I was never able to declare my interest. Being in Tampa was a chance for me to achieve my goal of becoming a part of the DST sisterhood, and as the confident phoenix I had become, I went for it! I wanted to serve my new community, and I knew that it would be easier if I did it with likeminded women by my side. Although I was new to Hillsborough County and didn't know anyone, I submitted my application and left it in God's hands. Well, they must have liked me because in the spring of 2009, I, along with eighteen other amazing women, became a member of DST. I was over the moon when I crossed, and my line sisters became some of my best friends. In addition, many of my other sorority sisters were also educators, and they wasted no time helping me become a highly decorated and respected teacher. As a child growing up in Miami, I never imagined that I would settle in and thrive as an African American woman in Tampa, but here I was, and I felt like I was on cloud nine. But in my euphoric haze, I ignored the crackling sounds of the embers and the smell of smoke from the flames that were on the horizon. I was so busy being happy, I forgot to prepare for the flames that were inevitable. For years I would pay for this oversight, and Tampa would just as quickly go from my place of bliss to a misery I couldn't escape.

New Flames

Tampa quickly reminded me that every level of life comes with flames. I came to Hillsborough County hoping to be the positive change I wanted my family to be defined by, but somewhere I forgot my nonnegotiables, and I was faced with issues that I never saw coming. Starting with my job! Teaching was a tough job, but being an African American woman teaching in Tampa came with a set of rules that I was unfamiliar with. Being a dark-skinned, outspoken, intelligent, and independent woman in my district made me a marked woman. Coming from Miami, which is a melting pot of cultures and attending a predominantly Black university for my undergraduate studies, I never felt like a minority. Being a woman and being African American, I knew I was a minority, but I was never made to feel like one. During my first year of teaching, I thought it to be a compliment when the students who were considered behavior problems were placed in my class. Because I grew up experiencing colorism, I didn't know there was a such thing as implicit racist bias. Overlooking Tampa is sixty-feet-by-thirty-feet Confederate battle flag, and although I am familiar with its history, I didn't realize how many people lived by what it represented. I didn't realize that, on my campus, I was nothing more than the Black girl who can handle behavior issues. No one cared about how much time and effort it took to manage these students, and it seemed that the harder I worked, the more they wanted me to do. I started teaching, wanting to make a difference and wanting to perform at a high level, and I was rewarded with more behavior problems.

It all became very overwhelming, and I started to suffer in silence. I would arrive to work while the bats were flying low in search of food, and I would leave when the custodians kicked me off campus. I attended countless trainings to become a better professional, and I made sure that I executed at an elite level. As a first-year teacher, I was constantly praised for my ability to manage my classes behavior and how well they were performing on their assessments. There was a list of parents who had begun requesting me as their children's teacher and principals who were wanting me to interview for classroom positions at their schools. I had become one of the "show ponies" on my campus, and my principals knew that they could count on me for anything that needed to be done at our school. I took pride in my work, and I enjoyed being known as a good teacher. But little did I know that while I was diligently working to be seen as an impactful educator, my district saw me as nothing more than a Black girl who so happened to be a teacher. I spent years working on my negative self-talk and reaffirming my self-worth (to myself) to now be faced with just being thought of as a Black teacher. I also realized that to some people being an African American woman meant that I was also considered intimidating and mean. I remember an instance when I was asked by my principal to come to her office for a conference. I thought that she wanted to place another student in my class, and I must admit that I had a bit of an attitude because of that assumption. However, I was disturbed to learn that I had colleagues on campus who thought that I was intimidating, and they confided in her that they were afraid of me. I was stunned to say the least. I made it a point to be polite and respectful to everyone I met because I knew that I was slightly socially awkward, and I wanted to make people comfortable around me. My principal, who was also an African American woman, told me that after working with me she knew that something was wrong with their statements. She said that when she asked them what I did to make them feel this way, they said that there wasn't anything that I did, it was just how I made them feel. I was extremely confused and didn't understand how someone could feel so strongly about me and I hadn't done anything to them. With the door closed, my principal told me that the problem was me. She told me that I needed to understand that I was a Black girl in Tampa and that in our profession, I would continue to encounter people who would see my intelligence and outspoken nature (coupled with my dark skin) as a threat. When I left her office, I felt myself change. If the color of my skin would determine how I would be treated, how could I ever ascend in this district? After leaving her office, I became hyperaware of my interactions with people (especially Caucasians). I was not accustomed to being stereotyped, so I thought that I could change how they saw me if I made it a point to soften my approach, raise the pitch of my voice, and smile more. I focused on becoming who I thought they wanted me to be, and somewhere along the line, I forgot to be who I wanted to be.

*****

I spent years trying to prove my worth to my district. I was exemplary rated by the district and the state. I was in my twenties and my body of work gained the respect of my colleagues, students, families, and principals. But it seemed that I was only good as a classroom teacher. Every time I tried to become a resource teacher, it was as if I was wanting to physically move a mountain. I recall once when I wanted to become a mentor in our district. Being a mentor meant being the professional that a set of novice teachers would look to for guidance. I wanted to help new teachers navigate their classroom and become the best educators they could. To become a mentor, I went to an interview, and after being screened by a panel of supervisors, I was sent on my way. I left feeling confident and thinking that I had a chance at becoming a mentor. In the hour it took for me to arrive back on my campus, I received an email telling me that I was not a good fit for the position. I was disappointed, but I was growing accustomed to being told no in my district. I went on with my life; but after about a week, I was approached by a teammate who told me that a friend of hers, who sat on the panel that interviewed me, said that I wasn't chosen because I looked like I fit the angry Black woman stereotype and that they felt that novice teachers would be intimidated by me. There wasn't anything that I said or did that warranted this perception, I just fit the mold. It was yet another dagger to my heart. I felt myself becoming more and more bitter toward teaching. I no longer felt like there was room for me to grow as a professional because everyone's mind was made up about me. I spent years giving my all to a profession that didn't seem to want me to grow and thrive on my own terms. To add insult to injury, my student loans were due, and I barely made enough money to live. I felt so defeated!

Chapter 10
Old Embers... Reignited!

As I continued to work to change who I was so that the people at my job would like me, I also had to deal with the old flames from my past. Now that I was a functioning, employed adult, I still desired to help my mom beat her addiction. She still lived in Miami, and one night I received a phone call from a hospital. I was informed that she was stabbed in the neck by two men who were trying to rob her and her boyfriend. They told me that they were given my number and wanted to let me know that she would be admitted for a while. While she was in the hospital, I traveled back and forth to Miami to check in on her and speak with doctors about her injuries. Eventually, I grew tired of traveling to Miami to help her, so (against my better judgement) I moved her to Tampa with me. I envisioned being able to help her get a job and become self-sufficient. I didn't consider all that came with housing an addict. Before I knew it, I became an enabler, and I learned why my grandmother wouldn't allow her to stay in our house when we were away.

My life had started to take a turn for the worst and forgetting that the life of a phoenix was cyclical, I was back where I started... Existing in Flames! I slowly fell back into depression and started having anxiety attacks, and in true introvert fashion, I became a recluse. I was back to my old self, and although it was uncomfortable, it was safe. I knew that it was time to continue my journey of healing by learning how to control the flames on this level of life, cool the embers, and prepare to rise from the ashes yet again. Step 1: go see a therapist!